Goodbye Good Girl

EILEEN M. CLEGG
SUSAN SWARTZ

New Harbinger Publications, Inc.

Publisher's Note

This publication is designed to provide accurate and authoritative information in regard to the subject matter covered. It is sold with the understanding that the publisher is not engaged in rendering psychological, financial, legal, or other professional services. If expert assistance or counseling is needed, the services of a competent professional should be sought.

Distributed in the U.S.A. by Publishers Group West; in Canada by Raincoast Books; in Great Britain by Airlift Book Company, Ltd.; in South Africa by Real Books, Ltd.; in Australia by Boobook; and in New Zealand by Tandem Press.

Copyright © 1997 by Eileen M. Clegg and Susan Swartz
New Harbinger Publications, Inc.
5674 Shattuck Avenue
Oakland, CA 94609

Cover design by Blue Design, San Francisco, CA.
Edited by Farrin Jacobs.
Text design by Tracy Marie Powell.

Library of Congress Catalog Card Number: 97-75475.
ISBN 1-57224-106-3 Paperback.

New Harbinger Publications' Website address: www.newharbinger.com.

First printing

To all the good women, generous and brave, who let us into their stories. Special thanks to Meg McConahey, our silent partner who knew when to speak up, and to Farrin Jacobs, our serene editor.

CONTENTS

INTRODUCTION

When she was good, she was very, very good, but when she was bad ... she had better stories to tell.

—Eileen and Susan

We carry around a lot of baggage, we strong, powerful, savvy women heading into the twenty-first century. Baggage filled with shoulds and pressure—from ourselves and others—to be what we aren't. Tucked neatly in the secret compartments are high expectations—to be competent, wise, beautiful, fit and young, a generous mother, supportive partner, pleasant coworker. We're climbing the ladder of success and polishing the steps along the way, then feeling guilty that we didn't do it better.

It's been more than thirty years since the Feminist Revolution opened new doors to the workplace, the political arena, and lifestyle choices. Intellectually, we know that our foremothers fought for our right to equality. But many of us still respond to "the rules"—often unspoken but palpable—about society's expectations of women. Having first met Virginia Woolf's "Angel of the House" back in a women's studies class, we are surprised to look around one day and see that we have become that unassuming woman who settles for the chicken leg and the seat in the draft.

For many of us, there remains a big gap between what we know and how we behave, because we're still picking up the subtle signals about what's expected of us—to be agreeable, with seemingly no complaints. We should be working to look and be the best: empathetic, good listeners, ready to lend a helping hand. While most of us value what's behind all that—the genuine desire to be liked and make the world a more comfortable place—the downside is discovering that not everyone is looking out for you in the same way you're looking out for them. Constantly trying to conform to others' expectations eventually saps all your energy until you're limp as a doormat and not exactly in the position to exert a positive influence on the world.

How do you know when it's time to change the rules? When you have a bold idea, but you're afraid to act. When you need time out, but can't find it. When you want to play, but hang back to clean the counters. When you detect a sprout of something that is the "real you," but you don't cultivate it because you fear disapproval.

The real question is this: How do we keep what's best about "womankind" without being the kind of woman who loses herself in the process?

Welcome to the Club

Answers come from the great oral tradition of women sharing stories. It's the chats over the washroom sink at work, on the sidelines at soccer games, and during late-night confessional phone calls that help us question our old behaviors and cultural attitudes. That's where we groan, laugh, and cry together. From each other, we find inspiration to make changes in our own lives.

This book began with a conversation between Eileen and an editor at New Harbinger Publications, Kristin Beck. They were walking on the beach one day, talking about how women struggle to be themselves amid all the cultural expectations and media images. Eileen's last book, *Becoming a Wise Parent for Your Grown Child,* encouraged people to look inside themselves instead of following social norms to redefine relationships between the generations. Kristin suggested a book just for women that would tackle the spectrum of outside "shoulds" that keep them from listening to the voice inside. How do women let go of the old-people-pleasing rules without losing the authentic qualities of compassion, thoughtfulness, and connectedness with others?

Eileen set out to find a compadre. As a reporter for the *Santa Rosa Press Democrat,* she didn't have to look far: Susan had been pushing the limits on women's issues for twenty years. Both of us regularly take on controversial subjects—Eileen in news stories and Susan as a columnist. But, at the same time, we secretly suffer from the Ms. Congeniality syndrome, except when we slip out of the office and remove our smiles. We grouse about work and everything else. We admit that our lives get messy—relationships and closets alike. We confide about the shortcuts we take to appear to have it "all together." We fantasize about ditching our responsibilities and doing something frivolous just for ourselves. From talking with friends, sisters, moms, daughters, and women we meet on the job—we know we are part of a big club.

In pitching the book idea, Eileen talked about the ethical dilemmas that arise when women reject the expectations of others in order to make room for their own vision. "Oh," said Susan, "you mean no more good girl!" That was it, we had our book.

Pretty soon we were listing all those good girl traits that get in the way of being your own woman. For example, being humble to the point of self-deprecating, cautious to the point of timidity, caretaking to the point of martyrdom, and, all along, trying to conform to society's media image of the ideal woman—young and thin with perfect makeup, a dream house, and a storybook marriage.

Then we thought what it would mean to transcend all of that. To ditch that automatic response that earns us a pat on the head. This isn't to knock some of the conventional feminine behaviors. They work as long as we're consciously using them to communicate what's really inside us. The problem is when those behaviors are knee-jerk reactions. Being too accommodating is literally self-sacrificing. Where do we learn how to keep that tender heart without turning to mush?

The Bad Girls' Bench

In our interview with Joy, whom you'll meet inside, we learned about the "bad girls' bench." It's where you go when you've removed your good-girl gloves. Been a little too direct, aggressive, disagreeable, or outspoken? Or, perhaps not cheerful, giving, or helpful enough? No problem, Joy says with a wink, take some time out on the bad girl's bench. It's where you go when you get tired of being perky. It's a place for your real self.

The bad girls' bench is any place where you have permission to laugh, cry, and kvetch. Here, you can be gossipy, think evil thoughts and, yes, be bitchy. It's not a place where most of us want to stay forever. It's a stopover place. A place for sorting out who deserves your good will and who deserves a permanent chill. It's a place to thaw the frozen smile and try on a frown. On the bad girls' bench, you can speak in four-letter words. You can rant against the toxic influences from the outside world and feel healthier for the purge. Beneath all those influences is your strong self, which can return to the world with some armor against the "shoulds" and a homing device that seeks true satisfaction in work and play.

Think of this book as time out on the bad girls' bench. To write the book, we sat down with women who have been letting go of some of their old behaviors and attitudes and we asked them how they did it. Then, in the interest of research, we joined a group of women who every year drop their responsibilities to be "selfish for a week" on a wild river trip. It was the first of our good-girl time-outs.

Our use of the term "girl," of course, is in no way meant as diminutive toward women. It's a catchall term for the old self-image that tends to keep us small. Most of the problematic traits we deal with in the book go back to childhood and adolescence. The goal is to outgrow, or at least modify, them—on our own terms.

Women's Voices

Many of the women in this book had epiphanies that transformed them and gave them personal strength to be themselves—not necessarily by choice. While some sought out opportunities for change, others landed unexpectedly in a crisis that forced them to reevaluate their old ways. They found themselves at the end of a rope and, instead of climbing back up, they decided to jump. In exchange for their candor, we offered new identities to protect privacy, jobs, and ex-husbands.

These stories are about giving up the safety net of being a good girl. But letting go doesn't mean a drop into the abyss. We might be ready to throw off some of the constraints that make our lives miserable, but we need something else to hang on to in the process. We don't want to go from being Snow White to being the wicked Queen. We want to find something in between that feels real. To do that it helps to get distance from our automatic responses. Then we can choose to take actions that express our real selves.

For the women you'll meet inside, letting go of the old rules meant rearranging priorities. For some it meant dropping a certain image. Others embarked on a major life overhaul. Sometimes it was just a small, interior shift.

The women in this book have looked deep inside, made choices, declared new loyalties, and risked the possibility that someone might get mad. They have overcome years of good-girl programming, retained what worked, and said goodbye to the rest. Each of us does this her own way, but it helps to hear the truth from others who have been there.

Today's challenge isn't just to gain access to new places in society. It's to gain access to the internal cues that will guide us past the expectations put forth by the amorphous "them" so we can create our own rules—rules that fit with who we really are.

Interviewing dozens of women for this book confirmed the lessons from our own experiences: When women start cracking the mold, we find ourselves drawn to others who have done the same. We can look back at our pasts with forgiveness, anticipate the future with newfound courage, and have some fun with each other along the way.

The voices in this book offer commiseration, inspiration, and guidance. Listen in. Perhaps you'll hear your own voice in the conversations that follow.

1

KISSING THE GOOD GIRL GOODBYE

Letting Go of Nicey-Nice and Finding Integrity

Don't compromise yourself. You are all you've got.

—Janis Joplin

Power is the ability not to have to please.

—Elizabeth Janeway

Let the world know you as you are, not as you think you should be—because sooner or later if you are posing, you will forget the pose, and then where are you?

—Fanny Brice

When Good Is Not Nice
and Nice Is Not Good

A good girl by nature, upbringing, and her own admission, Christine has a head of thick blonde hair, a sunny disposition, and a seemingly perpetual smile set in a face so beautiful she could have been a bad girl and still been forgiven. She's managed for most of her life to please just about everyone, and that has gained her a number of friends. Friends are among the perks that come with being accommodating, a good listener, and always trying to do the right thing.

But then there's the other part. In the self-deprecating manner good girls employ when they begin to question their others-first attitude, Christine confides, "Lots of times I've been a wimp." Much of her life has been nudged one way or the other by her basic deferential personality, she admits. "Life decisions have been based on my fear of hurting people's feelings." There's a good girl for you—submissive, taking care of the world, trying to please everybody and sometimes getting lost in the process.

Christine's ever-obliging attitude worked for four decades until the day she got pushed into a corner and had to take a stand. Public confrontation is the ultimate challenge for a good girl. And this one was of epic proportions. In order to save her grandson from neglect, Christine had to go to court to get the child placed in her custody. And that meant taking him away from her beloved but drug-addicted daughter.

Christine is one of those women whose drive to please others is so deeply ingrained that it took a crisis for her to recognize it. When something comes along that's more valuable than getting along with everyone, good girls are forced to reevaluate. The court fight with her daughter clashed with every one of Christine's instincts, and in the process she began to see herself more clearly as a second-generation good girl who grew up automatically following the rules.

My mother raised me and my sisters to be adoring women. You never say anything to hurt anyone's feelings. You are especially never unflattering to men. When my father came home from work we knew to be quiet. We took the backseat and understood that my father and brother were to have the exciting lives, the glory.

We took the backseat and understood that my father and brother were to have the exciting lives, the glory.

Takes One to Know One

It was during her life crisis that Christine began to see she wasn't the only one who grew up with those rules. Christine, an office manager, is efficient, agreeable, and a dependable bestower of positive feedback. One day Jane, who worked in the office down the hall, caught Christine in a shattered moment. It had been a rough morning: Christine's daughter had been picked up by the police again. After she got the news, Christine walked resolutely to the restroom, her stock smile in place. Once inside with the door closed, she gave in and began to cry. She was startled to see Jane, someone she'd passed in the hall but didn't really know. She caught Christine's crumpled face in the mirror and asked, "Are you okay?" Jane recalls, "Her eyes were already leaking, but she said, 'Oh, I'm fine.' Well, I recognized her type right away. 'Just fine' is our standard answer to any query about our physical or mental state. Don't bother anyone with your troubles. Typical good-girl syndrome. I couldn't help it, I actually started to smile and said, 'No you're not, you're miserable.' Then I told her that I do the same thing. I think I probably told the nurse I was 'just fine' in the middle of labor." The two shared a laugh; now they get together on a weekly basis and practice letting go of their good-girl routines.

"Just fine" is our standard answer to any query about our physical or mental state. Don't bother anyone with your troubles.

"Sometimes," Christine says, "I feel like everyone else is wearing a T-shirt that says 'Please Yield' and I do. I'm always giving in. The other day I let a man grab the gas pump even though I was there first. And I let somebody cut in front of me in line at the post office when I was already running late for work. Maybe they thought I was very sweet, but I felt like an easy mark."

So, what's wrong with letting some take cuts? Or not sending back the overcooked salmon? Or saying, "I'll have the vanilla, you can have the mocha fudge"? Or, "You tell me your problems, I'll stuff mine"? For one thing, you become invisible—not only to others, but, more importantly, to yourself. You give up your vote. Pretty soon other people stop looking to you for truth and you may even forget what it is you really believe. As Christine says, "The good girl doesn't really have to have an opinion, she's so accomplished at agreeing with others."

My problem with being the good girl is that I don't necessarily respect or believe good girls, so I'm always watching myself flattering people or giving in and thinking, "Please stop." But I can't. For a long time I had this feeling that in all relationships—romantic, business, friendship, family—you have the choice of being either the giver or the taker. And in my experience I'm the one saying, "You go first," and the other person is always the taker. The good girl is always the giver.

Of course there's nothing bad about being good. The world would be a better place if everyone were compassionate, good-natured, and agreeable. Those qualities contribute to pleasant interactions, companionable teamwork, and a caring environment. The problem comes if one day you look up and see your sunny vibes being sucked into a black hole.

If you're a source of light, others will be drawn to you. Some are kindred spirits, and you can take turns recharging each other, saying, "No, please, you first!" But all too often you encounter the other sort—people who are only too happy to absorb your energy and run. You stand aside. They whiz by. Suddenly, you're at the back of the line.

That's when it's time to reconsider all that modest, self-effacing behavior. It helps to talk about it with others who are also buried under a pile of the rules, shoulds, and worries. Good girls recognize each other. We share the guilt we feel every time we dare to put ourselves first. It hangs on our shoulders like an old sweater. We know that behind the obliging nature and the forced smile is a woman wishing she had the nerve to say, "Sorry, I'm busy with something else." But that would be selfish, wouldn't it?

"I think I grew up saying 'yes' too often," says Christine. "Then I'd regret it." When she and Jane get together, they practice saying "no." "I'm working on being 'un-obsequious,'" Christine says. They admit to their hurt feelings, their anger at those who take advantage. They take turns bragging about times they stood up for themselves. And they laugh over their often pathetic ways. Sometimes when good girls swap stories, it's like dueling marsh-mallows. Who's been the nicest? "I never refused any boy who asked me to dance," says Christine. "If someone asked me out I'd go if I couldn't think of an excuse quickly enough, just so I wouldn't hurt his feelings. I never went braless. I still can't gossip."

Jane thinks she has Christine beat: "I married the first man I slept with. I tell my daughters that frowning gives you lines, just like my mother told me. My friends in college called me 'Baby.' A guy I worked with renamed me 'Cream Puff.'" She pauses for a moment and continues, "My first therapist told me, 'I bet you always ordered vanilla because you didn't think you deserved anything better,'" Jane says. "My second therapist said it's really a conceit, this idea that I can make do, compensate better than others. So all along I'm thinking I'm just helping people out by letting them have the mocha fudge and the shrink says I'm con-trolling."

Jane claims she's overcome her automatic good-girl response:

> I realized that I was always saying "just fine" when peo-ple asked me how I was doing. Part of this, I know, comes from my great aunt once telling me that bores are people who tell you how they really are when asked. This reso-nated with what my mother taught me, or maybe an old

boyfriend or society in general, that you should keep your troubles to yourself. I think that good girls don't want to burden people with their problems. When good girls get sick they say, "It's nothing." Now if I have the flu or I just had gum surgery, I tell people. And, of course, I encourage others to complain away to their heart's content. A friend calls me the Mother Confessor, and it's true I've always been a good listener. People tell me stories. I guess I give the impression that I really want to hear and that I really care. And I guess I do . . . most of the time.

But continual perkiness can be a major effort and even resented by others. One of our good girls told us, "People ask me, sometimes with a bit of spite, 'Why are you so damn chipper?' So I say, 'It's an act.' What I don't tell them is that I've been on antidepressants for two years."

It takes a good girl to recognize how far another good girl will go to not make waves. Coincidentally—or maybe not—both Jane and Christine were married to first husbands who had love affairs with the women's friends.

Jane recalls: "They were both my best friends—my girlfriend, who was getting a divorce, and my husband, who I thought was so sweet for helping her get through a bad time. I remember when someone told me they saw them on the beach together I said how great it is that a man and woman can spend time together without sex getting into it."

Christine commiserates: "I knew something was going on. There were blatant clues. But I didn't want it to be happening so I told myself I was wrong." When she came home from work early one day and surprised her husband and her friend, both hastily smoothing their clothes, she couldn't deny it any longer. Still, she said, "I was so darn polite about it. No yelling, no accusations. In fact, we chatted nicely until she left. Later, after we got a divorce, he told me he was sorry he'd hurt me that way. And I said, 'That's okay.' What was I thinking of after all those years and all that work? It wasn't okay."

Jane laughs and gasps, "I know. You didn't want him to suffer any more than he already had."

"No," said Christine, practicing a bad-girl smirk. "Actually I did want him to feel worse. I wanted to put parts of him in a vise."

I think that good girls don't want to
burden people with their problems. When
good girls get sick they say, "It's nothing."

Flirting with the Bad Girl

One day at lunch, Christine shows up wearing a good-girl uniform—long-sleeved dress buttoned to the neck and pearl earrings. She sticks one leg out and smiles at Jane. "Bad-girl shoes." And they are—slightly trampy, in a middle-line department store sort of way.

Both women can remember growing up and sensing that maybe they were missing out on something. "When I was in high school," Jane says, "the hoods were the bad girls. I'd watch them. They weren't really bad people, like evil. They just challenged the rest of us and the teachers. They smoked, wore black clothes, lots of blue eye makeup, didn't smile much, slouched a lot. They had mystery. Good girls don't have mystery."

Christine recalls, "I never cut school. I didn't have the nerve. Isn't that sad?" It's obvious to any good girl why Christine didn't cut school. She would disappoint everyone from her parents to the school principal to that disapproving angel who rattled around in her head, the one saying "tsk, tsk" and waving a big, nagging finger. Good girls do not want to disappoint. "I think being a good girl comes from feeling insecure," says Christine. "You don't dare risk disappointing anyone or making them mad; if you do then you'll lose them because they count on you to be one way. If we aren't good girls who would we be?"

Christine and Jane both admitted to the one-time crime of shoplifting as a sort of rebellion against their goody-goodness. Jane stole a bra from a five and dime store when she was thirteen. Christine stuffed a camisole from a discount table into her purse long after she was old enough to know better.

Jane recalls, "We were walking through the store and I was looking at bras, although I didn't need one yet, and my friend said, 'Take it.' So I did and I'm sure that set off alarms all over the store because pretty soon a man in a suit came up to us. I'm sure I confessed and started whimpering as soon as he looked at me. Anyhow he let me off. When I ran out of the store, my friend was waiting for me. We were both terrified and that was the end of it." In retrospect, she reflects, "I didn't want the bra. It was kind of a lame attempt at having a bad-girl experience. I was terrified and thrilled at the same time."

Christine's motivation was more complicated, almost as if she were stealing something back from a world that had failed to reward her goodness. "I was mad at my ex-husband because he had an affair and left me a single mother at thirty. I told myself I deserved that camisole. It was plum colored and kind of tacky. But I had spent all of my small budget on my young daughters' school clothes and I was feeling resentful. I walked out of the store, miserable and sweating and sure I'd be arrested. I never did wear it much. I really never liked it. It was on a sale table." To this day, Christine can remember the cost. $3.74. Good girls remember their debt to society down to the penny.

Sensitive or Savvy?

When they start remembering the past, people-pleasers sometimes begin to see how much energy they've spent over the years tuning in their high-powered antennae. Many are so sensitive, they can pick up even the slightest hint that someone may feel uncomfortable. One day they come to see how uncomfortable they became in the process.

Christine recalls an event in junior high that didn't make complete sense until years later:

> We had to wait in line to get on the school bus and I was at the front when the vice principal held out his arm to stop us. His arm landed right across my breasts. I stood there frozen. I worried that if I stepped back he'd know what he did and he'd be embarrassed. But if I let his arm stay there he'd think I was a bad person. So I just stood there, looking away and hoping that he wouldn't be able to tell that I knew he was touching me. It might have been only ten seconds but it seemed like ten minutes of shame and self-doubt. I was horrified and humiliated.

Today she recalls that goody-goody little girl with sadness, realizing that even as she was suffering over the possibility that she might hurt another, a grown man was taking advantage of her passivity. "I know he knew what he was doing."

> I look back on things that happened to me just because I didn't dare to be rude or embarrass anyone and it really pisses me off. I was so locked in the good-girl trap, and some people knew it. We become easy prey, so predictably vulnerable. If men made a move on me I'd play dumb, pretend I didn't get it, rather than say, "Get out of here." Someone would corner me and I'd get away with a little nervous laugh. Instead of showing them I was furious, I'd say "hi" to them later in the hall. They got away with it. I had never learned how to look them in the eye and call them on it, so I always reverted to the good-girl stance of not making a fuss.
>
> There are a lot of things that happen that make you squirm inside. They cause ethical anguish because you don't want to hurt or embarrass someone. But you're getting hurt. There are so many times I should have turned to some woman and said, "Would you tell your husband to take his hand off my knee?"

Good Daughter/Bad Daughter

Christine had married her high-school sweetheart at twenty and not long after became a mother of two daughters. Monica was goody-goody and April was not. Monica became a cheerleader, and when there was any disagreement in the family she would literally stand up and cheer. "She hated arguments. It made her sick to her stomach. There'd be some tension starting and she'd jump in and say, 'Look at the new routine I learned at practice today.'" There's been a generational improvement on one important front: Monica, although a people-pleaser, knows how to handle unwanted attention from men. "She has limits," says Christine. "She's not the easy mark I was. If someone comes on to her she doesn't play dumb. She burns them."

Her second daughter, April, was, from the beginning, "forceful, sure of her rights. I admired her. She was charming and witty.

She wasn't timid like her sister ... or me. I thought. 'This kid will go somewhere,' and I wanted to cultivate it." Sadly, Christine couldn't keep April from sabotaging herself as she grew up. "She was using drugs and drinking. She had thuggy friends. She'd get into fights in bars and get arrested. She stole money from us. She ruined Christmas and Thanksgiving and birthday parties."

Christine always apologized for April to other family members, hoping that eventually she'd straighten out. Then April got pregnant and had a baby boy, Christine's first grandchild. "She moved in with us with the baby and her boyfriend, the baby's father, and it was awful. She wouldn't come home and then she and her boyfriend would fight and this little baby would cry and cry. April and her boyfriend would run out of the house drunk and get in the car, throw the baby in the car seat, and scream off into the night.

"I asked a friend of hers what the baby did when his parents screamed like that. And he told me that the baby would fold his hands and look down at them. It broke my heart." April would disappear for days at a time, leaving the baby for Christine and her second husband to care for. Then April would return and demand the baby back.

"One day she called me at work from southern California and said the baby was sick and I had to come get him. I told my boss I was leaving and drove straight there—it was a five-hour drive. They were in a house that was just trashed. They were all druggies. My daughter was stripping for a living. The baby had a raging fever and was listless. I brought him home and told my husband, 'We have to save this little guy.'"

Her daughter disappeared for some months after that, during which time Christine and her husband petitioned the court for legal custody. Neither April nor the baby's father contested and, in fact, didn't appear in court for the judgment. "Neither of them showed up. So I didn't have to confront her. At least not there," says Christine. She had reason to fear a confrontation. There had been plenty of earlier fights over far less important issues than this one.

> We'd gotten way beyond having a tiff with each other. One time my husband walked through the living room and thought we were wrestling, but April had actually attacked me. I can't remember why. It happened half a dozen times. She'd start hitting me. I'm sure she was on

drugs. And I would fight back, sometimes wishing I could hit her harder. I was so mad and scared. That was in the moment. Afterwards, it felt horrible. I kept saying to my other daughter, "This is not how families operate." I felt out of control. It felt so uncivilized. I was really torn. I had to make a choice. And it had to be the baby. He was the innocent child, not my daughter.

It was so sad. And public. I'd never confronted anyone before, let alone in court. The judge made his decision and we have our grandson until he turns eighteen. What I did was a contradiction to everything in my life, because I couldn't please everyone in that situation. I couldn't comfort everyone. It was the most difficult thing I've ever done. I ran the risk of losing both my daughter and the baby.

Her daughter is still troubled and addicted, but Christine holds on to the hope that one day there will be a place in April's life for her son. "I pray every night that she can be a happy person, but the role she'll play in his life . . . I don't know." She calls the judge's decision a bittersweet victory. "My daughter is a sweet and wonderful person. She wants her son but she doesn't. She feels the loss and that I betrayed her." Christine knows she made the right decision to go to court. "Every time I look at my grandson I know it's worth it. He's happy. He sleeps in the same bed every night. He's safe. He's not around drugs. He has his own little puppy."

Like many genuine good girls, Christine probably won't change her external mannerisms and desire to care for others. But now that she has become more aware of how much energy she has spent trying to keep everybody happy, she's less likely to make sacrifices that cost part of her soul and she's more likely to stand up for what she believes. "I've become pretty effective at championing the cause for others." When a number of her employees began to complain of sore arms and shoulders from long hours at the computer keyboard, Christine went to her boss and insisted that they either hire more people or modify the work.

"I might not have been able to say it for myself. But I couldn't stand the idea that people I'm responsible for would be getting injured without my trying to do something about it. When I think about it, my being able to fight for someone else is really about being able stand up for myself. It's standing up for my principles, and that's me."

The Ultimate Good Girl

Christine has begun to look at other women differently as she comes to understand how they often purposely turn attention away from themselves, even when they may need support. Inside, they're probably a lot like her. "You don't want to be a downer. You don't want people to feel sorry for you." It can be pretty lonely, being the strong one for everyone else and suppressing your own suffering.

Christine keeps in her mind an image of Jackie Kennedy following the assassination of President Kennedy:

> Jackie never lost her composure. She did everything right. Everything proper. But I remember one moment as she tried to flee the cameras. She was in the pink suit with blood on it and she tried to get into a car but the door wouldn't open. She had to wait. Just stand there until a Secret Service guy unlocked the door for her. I always think of that. Her having to wait, after probably thinking she could finally be alone and let go. But she couldn't. She had to hide her feelings a little longer. And the TV cameras don't blink. She had to carry herself just one more minute. And I imagined she was dying inside. The ultimate good girl.
>
> Given the opportunity to change some things in my life I would probably be a good girl again. What I wouldn't be is wishy-washy. You have to see the difference between that and being good. Some of my best friends are bad girls. They're naughty. They do things that are unconventional. That's the part I would imitate. Maybe I need to get an attitude. But I don't think being a good girl is altogether a terrible way to be. I don't like the goody-two-shoes part, but I like caring about people. I feel good when I go out of my way to help someone who's down in the dumps. It's good karma, like money in the bank.

I don't think being a good girl is altogether a
terrible way to be. I don't like the goody-
two-shoes part, but I like caring about people.

Extremes

Christine learned to speak up for herself without spending too
much time on the bad girls' bench. But other women do it differently, making the swing from good to bad before they find a
middle ground.

One woman who decided early in life to break out of the
good-girl mold is Justine, an attorney who these days can be as
bad as she needs to be to fight for her clients. Opposing attorneys
would probably be shocked to learn that at one time she was so
vulnerable and defenseless that her family called her "Sweet
Justine." As a little girl, Justine was shy and quiet and avoided
trouble—until life demanded that she get tough.

She was the middle child in a family of five, attended a
Catholic school, and loved the rituals to the point of play-acting
in church.

> I liked the female saints and martyrs. I identified with
> the nuns. I liked their lives, the way they made these
> processionlike movements around the convent. When I
> played in the church, I would fantasize about being one
> of those nuns, walking down the aisles with those big
> robes that would swish when they walked.
>
> Then I hit adolescence, my parents divorced, my
> family seemed to disintegrate, and my world kind of fell
> apart. With all the confusion, there was no real focus on
> me. I was known for making good decisions as a child,
> and my parents didn't think I needed supervision, so I
> was left alone a lot. Over the years, I'd felt the sting of
> my father's criticism, but now I felt unloved. At school
> I became a bad girl. I remember sneaking out of the class-
> room when the teacher's back was turned, going down

the hall to my friends' classroom. They could see me outside the door, doing cartwheels in my uniform, amusing and shocking everyone. I cheated, I stole and drank—just a little, all those things, but enough to feel the thrill of getting away with something.

Justine played girls' football, hung out with the guys, and was easy in their presence. She was rough and strong and could hold her own with the guys, and they knew it. She developed an attitude, and saw herself as different from those other girls who seemed so caught up with boys, so controlled by them. She refused to fuss over her appearance and make nice. "I was sensitive to what others wanted from me and felt the disapproval when I didn't conform, but I consciously willed myself to resist that pressure." Justine certainly wasn't going to be one of those good girls like her mom, who tried hard to please only to watch her marriage crumble.

By the time she was out of high school, Justine had learned to say "fuck off" and mean it. That was how she fought back against sexual harassment at her first job. By the time she left her hometown to attend college in another state, she had left most of that good-girl stuff behind. She became cautious about people who wanted something from her, questioning anything that hinted at manipulation. Her friends teased that she had more men in love with her than they'd ever dated. Justine's cool ways seemed to attract men. But then in her thirties, already established in her career, she met a different kind of man. Something between them made honesty, sweetness, and vulnerability seem not only possible but desirable. "My tendency to resist suddenly evaporated because he was simply irresistible. He really liked me, I really liked him, and we didn't have to pretend to be different than we were. For the first time, I was entirely myself but not alone."

Although there wasn't a happily-ever-after-ending to the relationship (she and her lover eventually parted because of overwhelming logistic complications), Justine cherishes the memories and what grew from that. "I became less cautious. I could be more open," she says. She found herself re-assessing all of her relationships, realizing she didn't need so much protection, especially from those who were deserving of her openness. And she created a healthy distance from the others. "I raised my standards."

The Next Generation
of Good Girls

Women recovering from a bad case of good-girl syndrome often find themselves worrying about younger women who seem to be following the same path they did. They want to grab them and warn, "Look out!" Although society's finally changing—all the classes about self-esteem and gender issue studies are starting to work—still, instincts remain the same.

Rosie, who's in her twenties, says girls are still giving in. "Good girls can really get in trouble when they're in junior high and high school if they haven't learned how to say 'no.' Then they're the ones having sex just so someone will like them. It's fine to be a nice, understanding person. But you have to learn to put yourself first."

Cheryl, the mother of a teenager, says, "My daughter came home drunk one night when she was fourteen and told me she was tired of always being good. We talked about it and I told her that I didn't blame her for not wanting to always be the perfect child. But I explained that she didn't have to do things that would hurt her or get her in trouble. She didn't have to be a bad girl. She could be a wild girl. She could do that by wearing something outrageous, or breaking into song. The good girl is pretty tightly wrapped. She can have a wild time just by getting goofy."

Getting Past Bad into Wild

The new outspoken Christine looks forward to exercising her strong self whenever she gets a chance. Who knows what will happen? Even her mother, who taught Christine everything she knew about being a good girl, has reformed.

"My mother used to put up with so much—from my father, from everyone. She'd never act out. She used to worry about what the neighbors thought. It was important to keep a certain image. Now she likes asserting herself. If someone makes her wait, she becomes snippy, starts drumming her fingers on the counter. And finally she's having a lot more fun than she ever did. She would never raise her voice before. Now she does. When the San Francisco 49ers aren't winning, she hits the TV with her cane."

Deciding a little letting go is a healthy activity, Christine and Jane now meet regularly in their own mini good-girl support group. They share insights with one another and find small ways to act just a little bad. Christine reports reading "that people like us get hemorrhoids if we've had an especially accommodating day." Jane quotes Carolyn Heilbrun in "Writing a Woman's Life." urging women to "make noise, to be courageous, to become unpopular." They send wine back. They don't smile unless they feel like it. They toast each other and consider their new options. Christine says, "You know, we could pull a caper and no one would ever suspect us."

2

"SHOULD" HAPPENS

Letting Go of What **They** Think and Listening to Yourself

Life is change. Growth is optional. Choose wisely.

—Karen Kaiser Clark

Think wrongly, if you please, but in all cases think for yourself.

—Doris Lessing

I cannot and will not cut my conscience to fit this year's fashions.

—Lillian Hellman

Schooled in Putting Others First

At her boarding school, Joy and her classmates were told to write out the words, "God first, others second, and myself third." They did this every day. Joy didn't think twice about it. She was eleven years old and already had that concept memorized in her bones. She was born into a family where appearances were paramount and, above all, girls must appear gracious. She began learning about good manners, subtle flattery, and constant attention to "what would people think?" in early childhood. It wasn't until she was thirty years old that she began to perceive what was important about herself beyond appearances.

In her youth, Joy was skilled in sensing what she needed to do to please others. The question "what do I want?" didn't come up. In retrospect, she says, one's self wasn't third on the list of priorities as she'd been taught in school. "I think one's self was actually about eighty-seventh."

The few times when something was important enough to Joy that her emotions burst forth to scream for attention, she was shut down hard and fast. She remembers one time in particular:

> I had gotten a very special dog named Sport. I adored him. Sport didn't care how I dressed. My mother was having someone to lunch, and I was home sick from school. The man pulled into the driveway in this large car and ran over Sport and killed him. I was standing in front of our large plate window and watching it all. I just burst into tears. I was devastated, and ran out and put my arms around Sport. I remember my mother running after me saying, 'You can't do this. You're going to make him feel terrible.' She meant her visitor, not Spot. She made me write him a note apologizing for my behavior. And I didn't even yell and scream at him. I was just sobbing uncontrollably. The fact that I couldn't contain myself was unacceptable to my mother.

What Will *They* Think?

The daughter of a socialite in a class-conscious Boston circle, Joy had an early and dramatic baptism into the other-directed life. Most girls do not learn the "rules" of society with the white-gloved precision with which Joy was indoctrinated, but they pick up on the "shoulds" through subtle messages transmitted between the lines of praise and criticism in daily life.

Many of us live with a vague but constant sense that *they* are hovering around us—invisible but ever-present judges watching us with a device that can tell if we measure up to the standards. The insidious nature of the "shoulds" is that they often dictate our behavior without our even knowing it. One woman said that at the age of fifty she realized she had spent most of her life feeling as though someone were watching her, to see if she was conforming to some standard she didn't fully comprehend.

The "shoulds" even plague women who have spent decades consciously resisting external pressures. One woman who was raised in a hippie-style atmosphere of liberation and vegetarian potlucks said she found herself giving a dinner party and worrying about a Miss Manners-like spirit hovering over the festivities and critiquing her choice of guests, menu, and cutlery. Her family had never really taught her the good-girl rules, but still she sensed their presence.

Joy was fortunate, in an ironic way. The rules that plagued her youth and early adulthood were so strict and blatant that she finally got to a place where she could name them, understand them, and confess with pleasure that she had failed to follow them. She freed herself, and can now talk about the Joy of Failure.

These days, Joy is an outspoken wit, a woman of substance with fiery brown eyes, red hair, and a penchant for the well-turned phrase. With the passage of time she has forgiven her mother, whom she wryly describes as "the reincarnation of Cardinal Richelieu." Her upbringing was designed to turn her into a woman of society, which she failed at with great flair, but her past experiences provided rich compost for growth into a woman who knows her own mind and doesn't mind speaking it.

Joy's tales of protocol are legendary among her circle of friends, as are the tales of her fall from grace. She has brought as much finesse to breaking the rules as others employ in following them. Joy is the one who taught us about the bad girls' bench.

The Original Bad Girls' Bench

It was with another fallen society girl that Joy discovered the place where she could begin naming her demons. Their bad girls' bench was a real bench in her friend's backyard, set back in the trees and hidden from the house. When Joy visited her friend, they would take time out and go sit there, smoking the cigarettes they'd sworn off, drinking wine, gossiping about shallow acquaintances, and making fun of the rituals that had once plagued them. "Can you believe it? My mother just sent me this elaborate filing system with all the birth dates, wedding dates, and childbirth dates of my sorority sisters so I could send them cards at the appropriate time." Peals of laughter. "I gave it to my daughter so she could play office."

Most of us don't have an actual bad girls' bench, but in order to distance ourselves from all the oppressive "shoulds" that stand between us and our dreams, we seek out similar venues—long talks with friends with whom we can be real, places we go alone to re-connect with the self, or a therapist's office where it's safe to unload resentments and fears.

For Joy, the memories of her past struggles have provided inspiration about what *not* to do now that she is a mother herself. She recovered from the shoulds of her upbringing with strength and vigor. She transformed her tribulations into dark humor. When she talks about her life as a fallen society girl, others see a bit of themselves in the confused and joyless little girl Joy once was, the child who was supposed to have the demeanor of a porcelain doll but instead had the exposed heart of Raggedy Ann.

If I had to come up with one phrase my mother crammed down my throat, it was "Be gracious."

Growing Up by the Book

Joy's mother was always concerned with how things looked.

> Before we walked out the door, I had to be dressed up
> like a parade animal with plumes on my head, crinolines
> and gloves and socks and ribbons in my hair, which is
> why to this day I live in sweatpants and I can't bear to
> get dressed up. I never want to be that uncomfortable
> again. There was so much emphasis on how one looked,
> what the proper uniform was. I never felt I measured
> up.

Joy was able to break out of the fussy-young-girl mold a little
when she took up horseback riding, something her mother only
allowed because it provided access to the right clubs and the right
people. "But of course I had to ride sidesaddle, can you believe
that? I even jumped sidesaddle. Give me a break." Joy loved
horses, but even in that arena, there was always the matter of
being correct and conforming to some external standard.

> My feelings were not supported. It was other people who
> mattered.
>
> Basically, the way I was brought up taught me that
> you don't have an existence, you don't have an identity,
> you're supposed to blend in and be a social chameleon
> and be a very flattering, reflecting pool for others. You
> don't have any opinions. You are supposed to think what-
> ever opinions someone else is expressing are brilliant
> even if they're diametrically opposed to what you pas-
> sionately feel. . . . If you have that kind of framework it's
> very difficult to develop any sense of self or self-esteem.
> Everybody else outweighs you, and their opinions are so
> much more valid than yours. It was true about all kinds
> of things.
>
> You were supposed to be very taken by certain
> things, old family names, things people had, houses or
> antiques or jewelry or whatever those trappings were that
> signified status. You were supposed to be extremely
> tuned in to those things and very impressed by them.
> And unfortunately, I don't know if it was deliberate or
> not, but I seemed to be very dense about what these

things were. So I was a constant disappointment.

Whenever I was sick, my father used to say, and my mother backed him up 100 percent, "Dead or dying, or don't speak to me." Anything short of that and you were being a whining, sniveling fool. And if I had to come up with one phrase my mother crammed down my throat, it was "Be gracious." There was this sense of always having to behave in a way that was almost like another century. . . . I hated it because nothing was ever true or honest. People were always responding to what they thought your social position was or they were reacting to other people with excessive flattery or obeisance to somebody just because they had more money or their family had been around for two hundred years or some other criteria.

I could never quite get it. I was really bad at boarding school—I think I still have detentions there—because there were rules about which outfits you could wear. We had to wear uniforms every day but then on certain days you had the dizzying freedom of choosing what color socks you could wear, but that was only on certain days, and I would always wear the colored socks on the days we weren't supposed to wear them and this was a really big deal.

But Joy still held out hope that she would please her mother. Somehow she made it through high school, earning good enough grades that, with her family connections, she was admitted to an exclusive but progressive women's college. Joy was ready to leave the rules at home, but was soon confronted with a whole new set of rules.

"I can remember arriving at college and my mother had dressed me. I was wearing a blazer that had yellow and green in it, and a green skirt and penny loafers. My roommate was there, and while my mother was still there, my roommate stripped off all of her clothes, picked up a piece of black velvet, sat down, and started to meditate. I could see I was several steps behind." Joy's mother was, of course, mortified at leaving Joy with a "naked spiritualist," but she had no choice. Joy was free.

But the habit of people-pleasing was so deeply ingrained that it couldn't disappear overnight. And it had become much more complicated. Her upbringing had not prepared her for the freedom of the late sixties. "I remember thinking, do I wear beads or not? It was okay not to brush my hair, but there was still the jewelry issue. Were my clothes too clean? There was a whole new world order of judgment about what you had to conform to. What was hip? It took me years to figure out how to dress, how to behave."

Her first marriage was to a man her mother had chosen, a young businessman on the rise, a member of the right clubs. The only telephone book his family needed was the social register (it included names and numbers of all the right service people). Sometimes, they even took their stockbroker with them on vacation. The ultimate status symbol. Joy had attained a social level beyond her mother's and she got an inside look at what it was really like at the top.

> If you can just glide by on your name or your money or your social standing, there's not much pressure to move beyond that. It becomes a very comfortable niche. It becomes like a time warp, with the same people attending the same parties and doing the same things. The people start to have a few more wrinkles and a few more pounds around the middle. . . . If you get to that level, there are so few people, you end up with this very small social group and that's all you see. Yes, you do have the dances and you do have the lunches, but it's the same goddamn people over and over again and you end up cannibalizing each other because there's no fresh blood.

She found herself longing for intimacy, genuine connection with people, but everything was about appearances—including her marriage. The marriage failed, and Joy had to regroup. She was neither interested nor comfortable with the path that had been outlined as the way to the top.

She began having days when she just really didn't feel like figuring out the prescribed way to present herself when she walked out the door in the morning. It was a slow process of discovery about what did matter to her. The first step was learning that appearances don't matter as much to other people as she'd been raised to believe. There were people like herself, people who sought care and affirmation for who they were, not how they looked. One day Joy had a revelation that helped her begin to break free of the "shoulds."

I really do think one of my insights came when I unexpectedly saw a man I wanted to impress. I ran into him at the grocery store and I really looked dreadful. Somehow I managed to forget about how I looked and just focused on him, and he came away telling everyone how wonderful and beautiful I was. I thought, "A-ha, people just want you to give them attention and they don't care how you look. My mother was wrong about this." That was the tumbler's move. I was about thirty.

I think it took me a very, very long time to grow up, not that it's a point you reach but it's an evolution of accepting yourself. I really don't think I was able to become who I really am—that sounds pretentious but that's the truth—until I had a child and I didn't have time to worry about any of that other stuff. For me, motherhood was the very best thing because it burned away all the unessentials. When people came by to see me and the baby, the house was a mess and I was a mess, but my baby was smiling and happy. It was fun.

These days, Joy lives on a ranch with her husband and daughter. They have big dogs that shed on the furniture, old horses that wouldn't get into the gate of a horse show, and lots of cows. Her daughter has science experiments scattered around the house. On the deck, she's growing fuzzy fungus things that smell strange and look awful but bring no end of fascination to a little girl with her eye on a future Nobel prize. There isn't much fuss about clothing. Joy shops at secondhand stores and estate sales. There are few obligatory social events: Joy just doesn't spend time with people she doesn't like.

I've decided life is so short.... I look back at all those people my mother tried for so many years to impress, and most of those folks are dead now. So what does it matter, that we got the note to so-and-so or delivered the flowers to such-and-such? You do that and you don't have time for the relationships that are really important. If I'm hooked on anything, it's having intimate relationships with people. We talk about real stuff, we're honest with one another. We say what we truly feel. There aren't the pretensions. I don't have the patience for them.

I think it took me a very, very long time
to grow up, not that it's a point you reach
but it's an evolution of accepting yourself.

Finding the Wants
beneath the Shoulds

Now, when Joy sends a thank-you note, it's because she's genuinely grateful. When she has someone to dinner, it's because she enjoys their company. When she gives a gift, it reflects real love. Some of the rituals are the same as those that plagued her in her youth, but behind them are genuine feelings, and a sense of choice.

In a conversation with a group of like-minded women, the consensus is, there's nothing wrong with being "nice"—as long as it reflects what's inside. And, in general, being polite is preferable to the alternative, as long as the rituals of good manners don't overtake your life. Lynn, an architect, says the "shoulds" have their place.

"It's part of the social contract we have with each other to have polite behavior. There's great value in being polite and having manners." Lynn is way past feeling that her life depends on being accepted by others, even though she feels a certain amount of finesse is necessary. Pleasantries are fine, she believes, as long as they don't prevent you from making your own way in the world.

When the Shoulds Collide

Even when women reach a point of integration where the "shoulds" and the "wants" are the same, they often find their lists of things-to-do spinning out of control. Your agenda may be packed with meaningful events—romantic time with your mate, volunteering for a good cause, time with the kids, meditating, exercising, pursuing your art, working toward a career goal. But the limits of time and energy constrict your ability to do it all. Especially now that people are coming to realize that quantity of time is as important as so-called quality time for maintaining relationships. Priority-setting is no longer a time management tool, it becomes a survival mechanism for self-preservation. One woman, not entirely joking, said she once had so many things to do that she made lists of the lists she had to make. But these days she only has one "short list" that gets her through the day. The short list focuses on what's most valuable at that time in her life.

Shea has a warm smile and a wholesome nature that draws people toward her. It's been a struggle for her to resist the myriad expectations others have of her. She's the mother of three children under the age of ten and a part-time assistant at their school. She lives in a small community where there are always other moms who need help, friends who want to confide in her, community events that could use an energetic volunteer, and social occasions galore. One day she realized that while she had structured her life in such a way that she could have time with her children and friends, all the attendant demands were draining her energy. She didn't want to be one of those moms who was too busy working for school fund-raisers to take bike rides with her kids. Or a person who sets the timer for a certain number of minutes per children's activity. She continually reminds herself that at this time in her life her family is paramount. And that means having relaxed time together, as well as time alone. She allows for hours at a time to go exploring or play with her children. She makes dates with her husband. To be at her best for her family, she needs to nurture herself. She takes some time for herself every day, exulting in the quiet of an early morning run. She schedules time for lunches and visits with friends who are important to her. But she is careful not to let her time evaporate with meaningless exchanges. Nor does she automatically say "yes" to everyone or make excuses for saying "no."

There was a time when Shea would have explained to a friend asking her to go shopping, "Well, I can't because my kids have their lessons, and then I have to tackle this mountain of laundry. I wish I could, maybe tomorrow" These days, she takes the shortened, direct approach. She'll tell a friend, "It just won't work." And she has learned to live with the looks of disappointment she gets from people who want more of her than she can give. For her, it's a better alternative than running around like a madwoman, trying to meet everyone's expectations and finding herself frazzled. "For your own peace of mind, and keeping your side of the street clean, you have to be honest," Shea says. "These days I get off on saying 'no,' without having to explain myself. It's not difficult anymore. I actually enjoy it."

Hysteria

An eye-opening experience for Shea was reading about nineteenth century women whose roles were laden with "shoulds." "The women back then were always having fits. Out of the blue, they would have sudden tantrums." After reading that, she began to step back and get some perspective when she felt overwhelmed. She remembers one time in particular:

> I just got back from a camping trip with my daughter. My boys just got back from an overnight. There were five suitcases of dirty laundry and the house was a mess and the next day was a birthday party for my oldest son. I was feeling crazy inside, totally nuts. I was screaming and ordering my kids around. Meanwhile, my daughter was picking bouquets of flowers, and I saw her being serene while I was in this frenzy. That stopped me. I sat down on the couch and told the kids I was all wound up and it wasn't their fault. Acknowledging my feelings to my kids felt like a good thing to do. It helped me and it helped them.

Feeling overwhelmed is a natural response to the feelings that come up when women get caught in a collision of expectations, when there's too much to do and it all seems impossible. The question is how to extricate ourselves when the "shoulds" come tumbling down around us. It's fortunate when women have close friends—or in Shea's case, sympathetic children—so it's possible to talk about the feeling of being inundated. That wasn't always the case for women.

Volumes of medical literature from the turn of the century are devoted to the "disease" of "women's hysteria." There was a time when women were to simply grin and bear it with a stiff upper lip, and do their duty in life. The word "hysterical" derives from a Greek word literally meaning "caused by the uterus." It began with the Greek term *hysterikos*, which means "suffering in the womb." In classical times, people traced many abnormal states to specific organs of the human body, and, since women were considered more unstable emotionally than men, it was believed that *hysteria* must be derived from some purely feminine organ; the uterus was blamed.

The dramatic opposite of so-called hysteria is following protocol, doing your duty in life, behaving as you "ought," and stuffing any feelings that come up in the process. Women who strike a realistic balance are those who choreograph their lives in such a way that they can pay attention to form and content—what they're doing and what they're feeling—at the same time.

"A really deep breath helps, if you can remember to take it," says Natalie. "The simple act of conscious breathing can provide a momentary break from the pressures that come up as the mother of a toddler, the daughter of ill parents, and a scriptwriter.

For Lynn, the architect you met earlier in this chapter, the trick to keeping perspective is to take the long view. She reminds herself that the troubles of the moment are ephemeral. "My favorite one is, 'Ten years from now, who's going to even know or care?' That works for me. I ask myself 'Who cares? Is this important?' Sometimes there are truly important things going on, but usually they aren't as big as they seem at the moment."

Coulda Woulda Shoulda

One of the most insidious aspects of the "shoulds" is the sense that you goofed somewhere, blew an opportunity, did the wrong thing, and now it's too late. Shedding the "shoulds" means accepting what is. And that can be difficult in the era of the megawoman. Even Joy, who got past the old-world social rules, still struggles with new expectations. "There are so many things that one is supposed to be adept at, I don't have the psychological and physical energy to do all these things. It's marvelous to have a plethora of choices, but on the other hand there are all these ways in which I'm just not measuring up. Maybe it was easier when the role models were more prescribed."

At some point, Joy took a deep breath and accepted where she is now. A mom and wife, a good friend, taking each day as it comes. She's come to see that if you spend all your time looking backward and kicking yourself, you could miss all the good stuff ahead.

The challenge is to let go of regrets, the roads not taken that we naturally assume would have led to a more exciting, glamorous, lucrative life. It involves letting go of the envy we hold about what we see as other people's perfect lives, those we assume are superior, more fulfilling, and successful.

Kim, who has had a number of careers from stockbroker to teacher, says that when she read Tom Wolfe's book *The Right Stuff*, she realized there are people, like astronauts, who plan their lives. "They go to the right school. They meet the right people. They plot their lives so that by a certain age they're in line to go to the moon or something. Maybe I blew it. Maybe I should have planned better. But it seemed to work out." She smiles and forgives herself.

At the end of the week—or at the end of the day—there are always things you might have done, might have said, that might have been. Some regrets have their place, if they lead to change. The others can go.

Some women have found ways to routinely cleanse themselves of the "shoulds" that clutter up their lives. Susie has a ritual for letting go of her regrets. She lights candles for things she feels she should have done, but didn't. "As I put a match to the wick, I envision what might have been different." She allows herself to feel what it would be like to have her "should have" materialize. She looks into the flame and contemplates what she wishes, in hindsight, she had done. After she experiences a full dose of sad regret, she blows out the candle. She watches the smoke that's left behind and asks herself if there's any part of that "should" she wants to translate into future action. If the answer is "yes," she takes immediate action—if even just a note to herself to remember something to do in the future. If the answer is "no," she forgives herself, lets go of the regret, and watches the woulda-coulda-shoulda disappear amongst the thin black smoke from the extinguished flame of what might have been.

Don't "Should" on Others

Letting go of the "shoulds" automatically increases tolerance. But it has to go both ways. So, you've had it with sending thank-you notes after every party. Fine, let it go. But allow the woman who loves those flowery gestures to have her fun.

Joy doesn't expect anyone, including herself, to follow the strict rules that haunted her growing up; now she can pick and choose among the niceties. When she wants to, she can produce a most elegant dinner party, write the kind of thank-you note that goes straight to the heart, or pick out the perfect gift for a friend. But the operative word is "want."

She's made slow but steady progress changing from "should do" to "want to." She is making the journey with the support of other women, a few tears, and a lot of laughs. She makes fun of herself and the rigid rules that governed her early life. When a friend invited her to a party, naturally she insisted upon bringing something. When her friend insisted that she bring nothing, Joy couldn't resist an ironclad rule from her upbringing: "One should never go visiting empty-handed!" On the evening of the party, she sheepishly appeared at the door with a plant and a note saying, "I know I shouldn't have, but I had to. You understand."

3

No More Weaker Sex

Letting Go of Being Timid
and Finding Your Courage

Avoiding danger is no safer in the long run than outright exposure. The fearful are caught as often as the bold.

—Helen Keller

You were once wild here. Don't let them tame you.

—Isadora Duncan

From Night Frights
to Night Hikes

"You know that part in the child's prayer," asks Janet, "where you say, 'If I should die before I wake, I pray the Lord my soul to take'? I believed it." Janet had childhood asthma, and the way people worried over her, death seemed like a real possibility. Later on, when she was a little older and living in Jacksonville, Florida, she expanded her worrying to nuclear war. "It was during the Cuban missile crisis. We had four naval stations in Jacksonville with nuclear-powered ships. My father came home from work one day with plans for building our own home bomb shelter. At ten years old I was having nightmares about nuclear holocaust. Now, it wasn't just that I would die before I woke up. It would be the end of the world."

There was always a part of Janet that longed to be brave, and as she got older, it became clear to her that she would have to overcome her fears in order to experience any excitement in her life. It took her years to uncover and face the monsters— internal and external—that were scaring her away from trying new endeavors. But she did, and now she leads night hikes designed to help other women conquer their fears of the dark and see the magic.

Like many women of her Baby Boomer generation, Janet was raised by parents who had been scarred by the Great Depression and World War II. "My grandparents had to leave their farm in Montana because of the Depression and a drought. The only job my grandfather could get was as a janitor. He had four daughters. They were all affected by the experience." Deprivation led to a wariness that became part of the family legacy. "I took on other people's fears," Janet says, "and it wasn't until I was older that I began to ask, 'Is this my mother's fear, my father's fear, or society's fear?'"

A fear of the dark and the big unknown prevents many women from moving forward. Getting over a basic fear of the dark is a metaphor for facing other obstacles. It is not lost on Janet, who spent much of her adult life conquering her own monsters.

Girls are less likely than boys to find themselves plunged into situations where the culture insists they show strength and bravery. As a result, many grow into women who shy away from experiences that challenge their physical strength and emotional bravery. They may end up missing out on everything from the fun of team sports, to the adrenaline rush that comes from barreling down a river or mountain, to the sheer satisfaction that comes from feeling strong enough to be brave for someone else.

For Janet, it has been a lifetime challenge to understand the nature of fear in her own life and among people in general.

Born Brave

Janet reflects, "I don't think that we're born saying, 'Okay, I'm here. Now I better watch my back ...' There's a baby picture of me at three months with my arms open, as if I'm saying, 'Hurrah, I'm on earth.'"

Before moving to California, Janet ran a nature program in Florida and she used to take preschool children on nature walks. From watching their interactions with family members, she began to see how innate bravery begins to disappear.

> Children who are three and four don't have any fear in the woods. They're all curious. But one time I invited the parents along and I had to stop the hike because every two seconds there'd be a new parental warning. "Don't touch that. That will bite. That will sting. That could be poisonous. Watch out. Be careful." And I thought, "So, this is how it happens. Out of love our parents teach us to be afraid to be alive." Of course there were many more warnings to the little girls than little boys. . . .
>
> I know that fear can overcome talent, creativity, and joy. We have evidence to support a lot of our fears. Bad things happen. But I wanted to be an example of someone who is not stopped by fear.

When Their Fears
Become Ours

Before she could lead others into the woods, Janet had to work through a number of personal nightmares. She realized how they were fueled in part by the worries of overprotective parents who, in the end, couldn't really protect her at all. "I think what my parents worried most about were other people. When I moved to the city, my mother called every week just to make sure I hadn't been raped or killed."

Janet first moved out of the house at the age of eighteen. A year later she was married. "He was gentle. I felt safe." That's one problem when women believe the cultural myth that they're the weaker sex— they sense that they need a man to protect them. But eventually most women discover that no one else can make them safe.

At twenty-one, Janet was raped by a family acquaintance. "I blamed myself because I didn't scream. I woke up. He weighed 250 pounds and he was crushing me." Her first reaction was to believe she had done something wrong, the result of years of cultural conditioning. "There were always reminders that you had to be cautious and if something happened maybe you caused it. I was attacked on the street once and the cop said, 'What did you do to provoke him?'" The attack and the rape were among many experiences that confirmed Janet's assumption that the world was a dangerous place, and she was powerless within it.

After Janet's first marriage ended, there were other men, and then a second marriage. She began to see ways that she had spent a lifetime conforming to the expectations of others and realized it was time to separate from that and find herself. Involvement in a twelve-step program for codependency gave her the courage to live alone for the first time in her life. "I was on my own without a man for four years. Before then I never let the sun set on one relationship before I had another waiting. I started feeling like this new person. I decided it was the essential me, who loved more than feared. I had a life. My body belonged to me, too. Not my parents or to the man I was with. It was safe to be an individual." She cut out a Rollo May quote about how courage is not the ability to live without fear but to live in spite of fear.

Safe and Free

As Janet began to disentangle herself from other people's constraints, she also began to connect with what had brought her pleasure and a sense of fulfillment over the years. These memories would help shape her future plans. "To me, nature was always God. If I was in nature I felt at peace." As a little kid she had her own playhouse in the swampy woods near her house. "I'd be out there all day reading by myself. My parents didn't worry about me out in the wild. They just didn't want me going to the mall."

She also began remembering long-ago night adventures with her father. The two would fish together, starting at dusk, and Janet learned to be comfortable among bats and other night animals. These were special times, and she felt safe in darkened silence.

Through her personal work, a vision emerged. "I wanted to help women walk through their fear. I wanted to take women into nature and help them feel safe, let them realize they belonged on this planet. My favorite time in nature has always been around sunset. I'm a naturalist, I'd like to think I'm a little like Thoreau, using part philosophy, part observation."

Fear is a biological protection. The instinct works to keep us safe. Fear itself is not a weakness. Letting it rule you is.

Friends with the Night

Janet began leading night hikes for women and was pleased to discover how many signed up. "Leading women on weekly adventures into the world of the night is the joyful way I make my living." She assembles small groups of women and, at dusk, leads them off on trails into the woods.

The night always works its magic. One woman said it was the first time she had held hands with the night and became friends with it. The more adventures I have with women, the more I love and admire us. We are breaking out and going where no women have gone before, and instead of finding out that our fears are true, it seems that fun, adventure, and friendship await us. I want women to learn to trust themselves and to trust nature. Part of it involves learning how to be in the present. I tell them, "The fear is in your brain, maybe your cell memory, but it's not here in the dark. . . ."

On one hike I had a woman along who told me at the very beginning that she had been raped. She was afraid when we came to the woods. I told her she didn't have to go through the trees, we could walk together instead across the field. But she said she wanted to try the woods. And she did. When she came out on the other side she was singing and she had an owl feather in her hair. The more fear you have, the more joy you feel when you face the fear.

Fear is a biological protection. The instinct works to keep us safe. Fear itself is not a weakness. Letting it rule you is. You don't stay out of the dark just because someone may jump out at you.

Janet feels that getting accustomed to the dark teaches women "to go forward even when you don't know what's ahead." On one hike, the group came out of a ravine to a meadow just as the full moon was starting to climb. It began as a skinny band of white light on a mountain. The group watched the moon swell into a huge globe that took over the hillside and set the coyotes to yelping and howling.

Janet tells her hikers that physiologically, fear and excitement are close together. "The symptoms are the same. The heart beats fast. Your body's awake. You're conditioned to be fearful, so you feel something and you think it's fear. But how do you know? Maybe you're just excited." She warns that when women start leaving their timidity behind, they might not always get applause for their brave efforts. It's still a threat to some people when women start getting a taste for adrenaline. "Little girls get attention for showing fear. They get put down for showing excitement."

Marianne bought a fishing boat and took on the Pacific Ocean alone after a boyfriend backed out at the last minute. Marianne was accustomed to detours and had been deviating for years from the path her mother had wanted for her. But the fishing boat was a wild yearning that topped even her brief marriage to a motorcycle racer after college.

The freedom of the sea spoke to Marianne. There were no fences, no limits, and no way for her mother to make calls in the middle of the night to remind her she was ruining her life. "I love being on the ocean. Of course, people told me I was crazy, but that winter I took all the boating classes, small engine repair—all of it. I prepared. Sure, I was concerned about all the things that could go wrong. I couldn't imagine anything worse than death by drowning. But my desire to be out there fishing and to be my own boss, going up and down that beautiful California coast, outweighed the worry."

Besides, she points out, her last job, a legal assistant, kept her landlocked and inside. "There was probably always a bit of fear, but it made it more exciting. When I was out fishing I was totally focused. My whole heart and energy was into fishing."

It took a while for Marianne to break into the traditionally male fishing community, even though she happily discovered she wasn't the only fisherwoman heading out at dawn for salmon and albacore. But acceptance into the once all-male domain finally satisfied a childhood longing.

> When I was little, I always wanted to go play cowboys instead of baby dolls. The boys looked like they were having more fun, going off into the woods and making noise. I pleaded with them and they finally let me play cowboys. But I had to be the cook. Being a fisherwoman, out on the ocean, gave me a chance to finally do what the boys did. It was hard work but sometimes it was so much fun it was like being a little kid again, and I was part of the gang.

When we are young, some of us love playing with baby dolls and some of us wish we could try cowboys, too. Then later we think it might be fun to play soccer, but we might get hit with the ball; or, it would feel wonderful to ride horses, but we might get thrown. We make the choice to stay in our safety zone and, eventually people stop trying to coax us out. As we get older it's easier to sit back and not go for it. We'll sit in the warm lodge and read while our daredevil friends risk breaking their necks.

Yet, secretly we want to be a woman who dares. So we look for ways to do it without taking on the killer slopes with the black diamond markers and we commit bravery in our own special way. For some it's a major lifestyle shake-up. When Sophie decided to sell her house and move to Mexico, hauling her computer, cat, and worldly belongings across the border and through the desert, friends shuddered and wondered how she could do it. "After the first hundred miles and nothing bad happens you stop being nervous." Now she is happily settled in a village near Guadalajara, in a community of Mexicans and expatriate Americans, and linked with her friends back home by e-mail.

> My shrink told me I'm counterphobic. When something scares me I go and seek it out. Someone else once said if a tiger is chasing you in your dreams you're supposed to turn around and ask the tiger what it wants. . . . I think if you're afraid to have an experience, you're not letting yourself be fully alive. Sometimes I'm scared and sometimes I'm lonely in Mexico. But I was the same in California and Michigan and Florida. I've decided those feelings don't kill me; they pass and I survive.

When Sandy made a tandem jump out of an airplane, the sky diver to whom she was attached advised that she keep her eyes open and looking up, even though she may have been more inclined to close them or focus on the ground. "The experience was thrilling and beautiful. Best of all, it gave me the message that there was nothing I couldn't do."

Solo Travelers

Traveling alone, or at least setting off alone, is another kind of adventure that builds confidence, even though there remains some social curiosity about the lone woman on the road. "Poor thing. Isn't she scared? Isn't she bored? I bet she's looking for a man."

Daisy has always traveled by herself on business, but on vacations she always tailored her travel destinations to spots where friends lived, so there would "always be someone there I knew." Then she took her first solo trip to Australia, New Zealand,

and Tahiti, where she knew no one, and it opened up a whole new world.

> Australia was easy, a good first destination, because when I was seated alone for a meal, people would sit down with me, even waiters and maître d's, but that's Australia for you and maybe not typical.
>
> When I am traveling alone on business I am much less friendly with people in restaurants and planes, but on vacations I've made some very good friends. I just start talking to people. It isn't hard to see something you have in common with someone; just complimenting them on their clothes is a simple beginning. If I end up by myself I fill in by writing lots more postcards and letters, taking more pictures, and writing things down, journal-style. I always have a book along with me for eating dinner alone.

She's now added Antarctica, Africa, Russia, Nepal, and Bhutan to her adventures. "On some of those trips I joined up with a group but I didn't know anyone in advance. My cabinmate on the Antarctica trip and I really hit it off. Since then I've visited her in England and she's coming to the States to visit me. I think you actually make more friends if you are by yourself."

On her Himalayan trip, Daisy had to split off from her travel group to come home early. "I spent one evening alone in Bhutan and was kind of feeling sorry for myself. There was airplane trouble and no way to communicate with the outside world. I was in this neat old hotel, and two women who worked there just came into my room to talk. It was lovely. They told me about Bhutan and I told them about the U.S. That wouldn't have happened had I not been alone."

Wild Women

Two friends, Martha, a travel planner, and Carol, a family counselor, formed a travel company specializing in no-hassle trips for small groups of women whose idea of adventure is more about braving the Paris metro than white-water rapids. They call themselves "The Wild Women," and a large part of their clientele are "recovering good girls" who used to believe that you shouldn't spend money on yourself, self-indulgence is selfish, and your families and office will fall apart without you.

Small-group vacations for women are part of the largest-growing aspect of the travel industry, and now just as many women take adventure trips as men. One woman who leads all-women backpacking trips said she thinks women get more adventurous as they get older and men are more apt to stay home.

The Courage to Stand Up for Others

Being willing to tackle new challenges can become a way of life, starting with one small risk and moving on to larger arenas. Some women may never experience a lessening of their fears, but learn to defy them.

In the 1977 movie *Julia,* with Jane Fonda and Vanessa Redgrave (based on the book *Pentimento* by Lillian Hellman), Julia tells her friend Lily that she knows she is "afraid of being afraid" and therefore might end up taking greater risks than necessary to not look the coward. Julia becomes the activist, fighting fascism in Europe. Lily stays home and writes plays but later finds the courage to go into Germany and risk her life to help her friend.

Sometimes it takes a crisis, when a woman perceives that she is the only one who can make a difference, to overcome fear. She must set aside her personal issues in favor of something larger.

Katie stopped seeing herself as a member of the weaker sex when she was serving on a jury for a young man seeking to be released from a state mental institution where he'd spent years for attacking three members of his family. "It was his yearly plea for release. If the jury agreed, he would be set free with no strings attached."

> Being willing to tackle new challenges can become a way of life, starting with one small risk and moving on to larger arenas.

There had been a few incidents inside the state hospital but nothing serious, and Katie felt in her gut that the young man was a victim of circumstances who showed signs of being able to become a responsible member of society again. "He was very likable, eloquent. He had a few black marks but I kept thinking, 'Where's the beef?'" When it came time to vote, hers was the lone vote to release him.

> I'd been driving sixty-eight miles a day to go to court. I'd become friendly with many of the jurors. The question was, did the district attorney prove that he would be a danger if he were released? And I said he hadn't proved that. I argued with the rest of the jury for two hours. This young man's mother was going to take him back home to the rancheria with her. He had a job. The mother was like a shaman in their community. I asked the others if he were a white guy going back to his house in Beverly Hills what they would think. I believed they were unconsciously prejudiced and that there was an underlying fear of this man who was big and dark and different and had a long braid down his back. One juror even said he wouldn't want to see him around any of his daughters. They said the mother didn't seem enthusiastic about taking him home. Well, she was kind of expressionless, but I felt that was her Indian way.

Katie was unsuccessful in her attempts to articulate her defense of the man. So she gave in and voted with the rest.

> They tried to soothe me that maybe he'd get out in a year. That he was safer in the hospital than at home. But I lost hope. I started to cry. I cried because I was mad at myself. I was disappointed at my weakness. They were all so damned unanimous. Once we walked back into the courtroom, I knew I couldn't change my vote. I hated myself. I hated all of them. My body actually hurt when I opened my mouth and said what I didn't believe. I went against myself.

But she made amends. After the hearing, Katie left the court crying, unable to look at the man or his mother, and ran into his defense lawyer. She admitted she'd voted against her conscience.

As a result, the young man eventually got a new trial, another jury, and was allowed to go home. Katie came to realize that even though she had taken an action contrary to her conscience in the beginning her compassion prevailed. Expressing herself, even belatedly, was an act of courage that resulted in a second chance for someone else. "I just know I did the right thing."

There are those stories about one hundred-pound women finding the strength to remove cars from accident victims. Eileen sometimes wondered if she would come through in such a situation. When the challenge came, it all happened so fast, she didn't have time to question her instincts.

Eileen describes herself as a worrier, with good cause. As a reporter, she's been at the scene of too many disasters and crimes. Although she enjoyed the occasional daring adventure, she had a fear of dangerous people. Then one day she was driving down a quiet street at midday when she saw an insane looking man harassing a woman and two children.

> My first thought was that he might be an abusive parent. My sister is inclined to march up and say something in such situations, but I usually turn away in tears. This situation was different. The man was yanking so harshly on the child's arm, and she didn't seem to know him. She screamed. And her mother started screaming. Someone had to do something.
>
> My instincts took over and I didn't think twice about stopping to help. It was like slow motion. I was acutely aware of not feeling afraid at all, but just doing all these mental calculations about the best way to proceed. I stopped the car and motioned to the woman to get in. She pushed the kids in first and was almost in herself, when he yanked her back and started beating on her. What amazed me was how many other people drove on by, ignoring what was happening, hearing the woman and me screaming for help. It looked like I'd have to leave the children and jump out to help the mom. But then finally a man stopped and ran over to help the woman. The attacker abruptly stopped and started walking away as though nothing had happened.
>
> Later I learned that the man was schizophrenic with a history of violence. He had been hallucinating. This wasn't the first time. He had almost killed a woman in

Texas the same way. This woman, he only bruised, but because of this assault he was convicted of attempted murder and sentenced to an institution for the criminally insane.

The police honored me as a heroine, and that was kind of exhilarating. Fighting the good fight and winning. I'd always carried around a little of my self-image from elementary school as the littlest in the class, but I found out that power doesn't have to do with size. It has to do with being willing to take risks for a good cause. I'm less afraid now, physically and in other ways. I'm not as easily pushed around by others. I believe that my courage will always be there when I need it.

There's power in letting go of the good-girl stereotype that tells us to mind our own business and rationalize not getting involved when others are in trouble. The world becomes a safer place when women feel strong enough to fight for themselves and others. We become part of an evolution toward a healthier society.

Nancy has made a career out of making the home a safer place for women, and that has required the personal strength to deflect criticism from people who would rather not deal with the issue of domestic violence.

An attorney who lectures at a prestigious law school and writes legal textbooks on domestic violence, Nancy often appears before her state legislature to lobby for bills aimed at protecting women and punishing offenders. She also gives trainings for police officers who respond to 9-1-1 calls. Her legal research and writing has resulted in changes in laws in the United States and inspired women's advocates in Germany and China, where she has lectured and worked with women's groups. She might have chosen the more lucrative mainstream route of private legal practice or tenure track as a law professor, but instead maintains a low-budget office at home, where she lives with her husband and son, allowing herself the freedom to choose her own direction.

I found out that power doesn't have to do with size. It has to do with being willing to take risks for a good cause.

"I really do believe that working to stop domestic violence is a big liberation for women and I want my life's work to be something that will make a difference in the world. That's much more important to me than being famous or making money or getting people's approval," Nancy says.

Not only does she often fail to get approval, she has sometimes experienced public ridicule for her work. After public hearings on a bill that would punish spousal rape equally with other forms of rape, a state senator got personal with his disagreement. "He was quoted as saying the state didn't belong in the bedroom and he had never heard about spousal rape. He argued we should completely decriminalize it. Later he said to the press that the women who were advocating for the new law were a 'bunch of ugly women no man would want to touch.' My response was to laugh and make copies of his quotes, give them to my friends and joke about them."

Her friends got a good laugh, agreeing that the senator's comments could not have been more ridiculous. She wasn't even tempted to respond to the insults. "We felt sure enough of our position, we didn't need to stoop to that," she says.

Raised by a minister father and social activist mother, Nancy was brought up to strive for more than approval in the moment.

> I was brought up believing that social justice was the most important goal. . . . It's important to decide what you really want to see happen and keep going for that, no matter what people around you say. The biggest reward for me is the statements battered women have made to me. Once, after I got finished testifying as an expert witness in court, a woman came up to me and said, "I'm pressing charges against my husband and what you said has given me the strength to keep going. And when I get through with this part of my life, I want to talk to other people about domestic violence."

Nancy has become a role model for others who want to make a difference. "I tell people, you can hold on to your dreams. Don't give up and don't settle."

The most important thing is to decide what
you really want to see happen and keep
going for that, no matter what people
around you say.

Getting Sweaty

Confidence can come from taking risks and pushing yourself to
the limit, and there's a growing awareness of how sports help
girls to develop that confidence. Timid girls, however, don't always
jump in, especially if they were born before Title IX, the 1972
equal rights action that forced schools in the United States to give
girls as many opportunities as boys to participate in sports.

A lot of women look back and realize the gym door got
slammed in their faces before they had a chance. Today they're
likely to look at women like hoops whiz Sheryl Swoopes and
runner Jackie Joyner-Kersee with envy, hoping that in their next
life they'll get to be a jock.

Sports can be tough for some women. They think they have
to be natural athletes to participate. Or they're still suffering from
their old gym class days when their teacher made fun of them
for not being coordinated, or they were the last to be picked for
the team. There were, of course, special girly-girl points for not
being athletic back then. It was okay if you didn't make the team
because the dominant culture would rather have you be a cheerleader, and if you didn't make that squad at least you could sit
prettily in the stands and wave your pompoms. But then one day
you wished you had learned how to throw a ball overhand and
that you could be part of a team that got sweaty and dirty and
went on overnight bus trips to visiting schools.

Penny started playing sports to shape up after the birth of
her third child. First she tried tennis. "I felt a whole new me
beginning to emerge. At first I merely enjoyed being outside, with
other women, learning a new skill. Then I let my competitive self
kick in and loved improving, winning a few matches, the good

sense of fatigue afterwards. I had a hard time with winning though, and I think that was and maybe still is cultural or societal. Nice girls aren't tough; nice girls try to make other people happy."

Then she went to soccer. "Boy, did things change. We ran at the ball, into each other, tripped, got kicked and elbowed, fell in the mud. God, it was fun. Some women were frightened by the confronting nature of the game. When two people go for the same ball, there is a good chance you're going to bang into each other unless one person backs off. But I loved it. It's not only physical, it's mental."

And psychological. She says, "I feel stronger for being active and more confident. I feel like I command more space than I would if I didn't play sports."

One of the greatest benefits for Penny was her realization about the importance of such activities for young women in to-day's world. "The beauty of girls participating in sports is that they learn their bodies are useful rather than merely ornamental. They learn that it feels good to sweat and breathe hard. They learn their hair can get messed up, their knees scraped, their clothes dirty. They learn about camaraderie and competition—that you can play hard against someone, then after the game, slap backs and eat orange sections together."

We could blame it on society for wanting us to stay feminine, which meant clean, neat, and passive. Or the boys for wanting us to cheer them on instead of vice versa. Or our mothers for telling us we shouldn't be tomboys.

But we did it to ourselves, too. Some of us just didn't try hard enough, didn't want to risk looking foolish or making mis-takes, so we lost our opportunity. Jane, a child of the 1950s, tells her story, but the same words could describe her daughter's ex-perience decades later. When it came to sports participation, both of them stepped away from the plate when they found they couldn't easily succeed.

> When I was in grade-school gym class, I had to stand in line and try to shoot a ball into a basketball hoop until it went in. Aim and throw. Over and over. It never went in. I spent a long time, in my memory at least the entire gym period, trying to do it. I start to sweat and maybe even to tear up just thinking about it. I decided that day that I was never going to be any good in athletics. When

I got into junior high I almost changed my mind because I was beginning to like volleyball. Then one time the ball bounced off my head. I was mortified. I could have laughed, made a joke. Everyone else did. But that confirmed once and for all that I couldn't do sports. Even when someone pressured me to try, I always expected to blow it. It has happened with sailing, golf, riding horseback, tennis, golf. The only sport I'm good at is aerobics. That's my little joke. But if I'm good at aerobics then that means I am nimble and I am strong and I am coordinated. This means I could have played sports if long ago I had let go of those humiliations. I gave up on my confidence in one area that I can now see gives many women much pleasure.

The beauty of girls participating in sports is that they learn their bodies are useful rather than merely ornamental. They learn that it feels good to sweat and breathe hard.

Starting Now

For many women, taking up a new form of physical activity later in life assuages some of those old feelings of loss.

Linda always wished she'd been more physical when she was in her teens and twenties. But she's not missing out anymore. She got involved in an organization called Coastwalk that holds a twenty-one-day beach-to-beach hike every summer. They traverse four counties along the Pacific coast. Linda found herself keeping in shape throughout the year in preparation for the sojourn and soon discovered she had a penchant for the physical.

"I sure do love exercise at this age. When I grew up, there was no organized physical activity for girls in school. My mother let us know that we were the smart kids, and that brains were what mattered, not sports. I tried to feel superior, not rejected, when I couldn't hit a softball or sink a basket in occasional school recess games. I wonder what it would have been like to participate in sports all my life."

4

LIKING WHO'S IN THE MIRROR

Letting Go of the Media Ideal and Finding Your Radiance

It matters more what's in a woman's face than what's on it.

—Claudette Colbert

Our vanity is the constant enemy of our dignity.

—Anne Sophie Swetchine

Lookin' Good

Helene walked into the party with shoulders straight and curves accentuated by silks. At nearly fifty, she was a women who turned heads, and this was no small source of confidence and pleasure after decades of unhappiness with her looks. Blessed with an un-wrinkled complexion, a lively wit, and the energy of a teenager, she was often mistaken for someone a decade or more younger. She had given her scale to Goodwill, declaring that she no longer needed the tyrannical object in her life. Along with the scale, she'd given up the mental ticker-tape that had chanted "I'm-too-fat-I'm-too-fat-I'm-too-fat" since her mother had put her on her first diet at the age of seven. Now she felt light and attractive, at home in her body—five-foot-eight and strong. She had shed some thirty pounds over the past year, but more importantly, she had shed the goal of looking like anyone other than herself. Although she'd always had a profound aversion to the media-driven image of beauty, she confesses, "Though I knew it intellectually, I didn't know it emotionally." She found herself adhering to the traditional image of beauty, which didn't look anything near age fifty. "I'd dyed my hair for twenty years. It was my big lie."

The Big Lie

Most women have their own version of "the big lie." There's noth-ing intrinsically wrong with coloring your hair or any other cos-metic trick you enjoy. Cosmetic surgery may be a solution for some people, where just a little blush will work for others. Women have been decorating themselves forever. The challenge is to figure out how much of it you're doing for yourself—and how much you're doing it to try and measure up to somebody else's idea of how you should look. Whose standard is it? A man's? A maga-zine's? Your mother's? Or your own?

Helene's lie involved striving for an image that was ten to fifteen years younger than her actual age—even when that meant compromising the real picture of her life. For some women the lie may be more dangerous, like throwing up their meals so that they don't take in calories and in the process, robbing themselves of nutrition. For still others, the lie may just be a little white one. For generations, curly-locked women have straightened their hair and lank-haired women wrecked their hair with too many perms. From potentially dangerous implants that make your breasts perky to cream that supposedly fades wrinkles, the beauty industry claims to satisfy the full range of women's insecurities about their appearance. The advertising is blatant. "Escape Your Shape," screams a Cosmo cover. Not exactly a self-affirming message.

Helene's beliefs are shared by many women. "We're in a totally youth-focused society. Women are not valued after they're forty. They're valued when they're young. Maybe it's biological, because that's the age when they can still make babies, or maybe it's that women suspect that they become more threatening to men as they age. When women get older, they don't appear nearly as vulnerable, malleable. I confess. I wanted to look young to please men." She says the pressure to look young doesn't afflict just women in midlife—women begin to check for forehead wrinkles in their twenties.

Helene is no longer a slave to magazine directives, and has spent years learning to appreciate her natural beauty. While she enjoyed her red hair, it became a symbol of not fully accepting herself.

"Escape Your Shape," screams a Cosmo
cover. Not exactly a self-affirming message.

Feeling Bad

Helene's mind-set was not uncommon, but she was uncommonly determined not to be stuck with it. It was a long process, one that ended up transforming her in ways she didn't expect.

She had spent many years feeling ill at ease in her own skin. Raised by critical parents, Helene struggled all her life to feel worthy. In recent years, she had come to see how fat had fed on depression and depression had fed on fat. "I used to starve myself and then binge. I really believed that if I just lost twenty pounds, suddenly everything in my life would be better. One time I went into a hospital for a weight-loss program and I spent the whole time in there planning what I'd eat when I got out."

Exercise turned out to be the solution to the dual problems of fat and depression. Since her mid-forties, Helene had gradually added more pieces to her exercise regimen. "I lifted weights, did Tai Chi, and walked, several times a week for hours at a time. Taking a long walk along the San Francisco marina replaced long lunches as a social event."

An internal change was occurring as well. Her own health, strength, and grace were superseding the Cindy Crawford standard for beauty. "I think it begins from within. It's about loving yourself. If you can start feeling self-acceptance and self-love, you'll begin to feel more beautiful."

Attracting Younger Guys

At the party, someone introduced her to a handsome young man who might have been thirty-five, and they struck up a conversation. There was a time in her life when Helene might have been suspicious of his interest in her. "I used to indulge in the 'what's-wrong-with-him-if-he's-interested-in-me' syndrome. You know, 'I didn't want to be a member of any club that would have me as a member.'" But she was moving beyond those days of questioning why a man would give her attention. She was starting to understand what others saw in her. "Friends would tell me that I'm attractive and warm and caring." She laughs, "One told me I had a nice butt." Slowly, Helene was beginning to believe them and to appreciate what her friends saw in her wide-set brown eyes and felt in her strong presence.

She warmed to the gentle presence of this man, letting him know that she was single, and she felt an open, comfortable response—until the conversation turned to personal lives. "Do you have children?" he asked. "Yes, two." Her stomach turned as she anticipated the next exchange. Would he ask their ages, and would she tell him that her daughter was almost thirty? Although she was becoming more comfortable with herself, she was still not anxious to let potential suitors know that she was not as young as she looked. She had worked for her youthful looks, why shouldn't she enjoy them? She managed to steer the conversation away from the subject of children, but she was left feeling that something was not quite right. "I always thought I should lie about my age." Now she wanted to be confident enough to own up to her age, to be proud of the fact that she had two delightful grown children. And that meant leaving behind her big lie.

The Big Breakthrough

"When I hit my fiftieth birthday, I really came into a wonderful part of my life. I felt a sense of accomplishment at having come this far, at having survived. It was almost as if I had permission to be my age. I no longer wanted to deceive people." One day, Helene recalls, she was out at lunch with a group of friends. "We all had the same reddish tone to our hair," which, she said, struck her as somewhat bizarre. Helene had gotten her first streaks of gray in her twenties and started early with henna to cover it. It worked. She looked perpetually younger than her years. Her son and daughter grew up watching jaws drop when Helene introduced them as her children. In recent years, they even had, on occasion, agreed to pretend they were younger than they were. It was an inside joke.

One day, Helene's daughter turned to her and said, "I love the natural look of women in their fifties." She paused for a moment and then continued, "Why don't you let your hair go gray?" Her children's opinions had always been important. Shortly after her fiftieth birthday, Helene realized that she was finally ready to let her hair return to its natural color. The change symbolized an internal shift, as well as an external statement of self-acceptance.

> I realized how, in the past, I had judged my life and my daily activities based on "Did I do it right?" Or, "Did I offend anyone?" As I realized that what mattered was how I felt about myself, I began to look in the mirror

and see that my red hair somehow didn't match the rest of me. The change wasn't sudden. I went over a period of nine months to a hairdresser who gave me a reverse weave that allowed the gray to emerge bit by bit, until eventually my hair was its natural color. The result was great. I didn't have any idea it would turn out so well or that others would respond so well.

Helene ended up with thick, naturally streaked hair, dramatic white swaths amid charcoal-gray and black. More than one friend asked if she had paid to get those streaks. Helene loved the way it looked and felt. She got a new cut that gave her a fresher look than she'd ever achieved with the auburn tresses. Her children were elated, and when she looked in the mirror she felt she was seeing herself for the first time. "My hair and my face matched. It looks softer." She found herself with a new level of confidence. "This is me with gray hair. This is me."

The reactions from men were surprising. "I ended up getting more action with men," she says with a laugh. She still turns heads when she walks into a room. That was something she had not anticipated. When she meets someone new, she feels more like herself—more open and accessible. She doesn't need to lie about having children in their late twenties. There's no doubt that her attractiveness now runs deeper, probably in part because she feels at ease with herself.

People still tell Helene that she looks younger than her age, but she no longer considers that a measurement of her beauty. "I realized one reason I had been coloring my hair was because I wanted to appeal to younger guys. As it turns out, they're not so stuck in their stuff, not so macho and set in their ways as I thought."

Nor could she have anticipated the responses from friends. "There was something remarkable about how letting my hair go gray has affected other women." At first, friends would tell her it looked good, but in the next breath they'd say things like, "But I'm not ready yet." People see her decision to go gray as a statement of self-acceptance. And women her own age see it as a challenge—a challenge they may not be ready for quite yet. Helene makes sure not to impose her choice on others.

The reaction from her therapy clients has been mixed. "One of my clients told me I looked like I was getting older. I just smiled and said 'thank you.' I don't think my patients see me as a glamour queen. But they do see me as a role model."

Resisting

The beauty industry has made billions on making women feel inadequate. Ads for everything from ice cream to cigarettes carry the subtle message that using their product will make us appealing to men and the envy of other women. It may be an ad for perfume, but the selling tool is the equation we all know by heart: slimness + youth = sex appeal.

The advertising is working— all too well. Even before girls are getting buds on their breasts, they are obsessing about their waistlines. Girls in the United States become serious dieters by the fourth grade. It's shocking to mothers who are struggling with their own self-image issues to they realize that their prepubescent daughters are heading down the familiar road to body-hate. "When I start to complain about my thighs, I go in the bathroom and close the door," says one mother.

Justine has waged her own personal campaign against media stereotypes. She refuses to wear makeup or pantyhose or anything else uncomfortable. "I've always liked knowing people were attracted to the real me," she says. At one point in her life, Justine even screened her suitors by dressing down—wearing jeans or sweatpants—for the first few dates.

It's ironic when women of all different shapes and sizes talk with one another and realize that through the years we have all twisted ourselves to conform to the same ideal. And it's liberating to realize that perhaps the ideal doesn't exist at all, except in our minds and in the fantasy photographic magic tricks that make models look the way they do.

The Truth Behind
the Obsessions

When women begin telling the truth about their beauty obsessions to one another, we begin to see how, through our silence, we have been perpetuating their big lie. Where did it start, this striving to look like someone else?

Helene was a slim and attractive little girl, with a bit of little-girl chub, when her mother decided it was in Helene's best interest to lose some weight. That decision kicked off decades of roller-coaster dieting, bingeing, starving, and intermittent bouts of self-loathing and self-restraint. Feeding herself was forbidden, and when she did it, it was with a vengeance. Then she'd pay by starving, which was all about pleasing others. In retrospect, Helene can see that it was all part of the good-girl syndrome; she was busy worrying what "they" would think.

"They" call out to us from the front of magazines in the checkout line at the supermarket, from the television commercials, and from the between-the-lines anxiety we hear in conversations with one another. It's ironic when women of all different shapes and sizes talk with one another and realize that through the years we have all twisted ourselves to conform to the same ideal. And it's liberating to realize that perhaps the ideal doesn't exist at all, except in our minds and in the fantasy photographic magic tricks that make models look the way they do.

If there were truth in advertising, perhaps the warning label on the latest get-thin-quick product would read something like this: "Forget it! You'll never, ever look like this because this model doesn't really look like this either. Every wrinkle and mole has been airbrushed away and digital photo retouching has shortened her nose, whitened her eyes, even reshaped her hips. Those are another model's hands grafted on, and those breasts are made from silicone. See how they don't move when she runs or lies down? To maintain her emaciated look, she trades smoking for food and when she does eat she throws up. Her bones are already so weak that by the time she's forty-five she'll have osteoporosis."

Anne talks about how she tried to get her already-slim ten-year-old granddaughter to quit studying the sides of food containers for fat content. "If you eat what's healthy, you'll look like you're supposed to look. Like your own healthy self." Beloved as it was to the little girl, her grandmother's voice could not eclipse the din of the media messages the little girl has been hearing for most of her life. The little girl gave Grammy a circumspect raise of an eyebrow and a twitch of the mouth that silently communicated, "yeah, yeah, yeah." Anne searched her mind for a metaphor that might work. The girl loved dogs, so Grammy asked her, "If you had a golden retriever, would you wish it looked like a basset hound?" Her granddaughter laughed and shook her head. Anne continued, "People are like dogs in that way; we're meant to come in different shapes and sizes, with different colored hair and eyes. You wouldn't want a Jack Russell terrier to have more curves, and you wouldn't want a sheepdog to go on a diet!" The little girl laughed and tilted her head thoughtfully. It was a small step, but nonetheless one that seemed to leave an impression.

Do I Look Fat?

With a grimace, Helene confides her regret over the number of times, when her children were small, that she would get dressed and stand before her kids asking, "Does this make me look too fat?" Or, "Do I look okay from behind?" At that time, low self-esteem was not a topic of general concern.

Helene's children had lived with her through her insecure days, but they also were witness to her transformation. "I was in bad shape and I changed. They saw this metamorphosis and began to see me as strong and capable." The change was slow, unfolding over decades.

Helene went back to school in her thirties and got her counseling degree in her forties. Through her psychotherapy practice and in her life, she began to see that it was more common than not for women to have deep angst over their physical appearances, and that angst could be discussed in the intimate setting of therapy or in conversations between close friends. The ultimate bonding between two women seemed to be "popping the question." The question goes something like this, in a low whisper: "Now tell the truth, how do I really look?" Women seemed to be constantly looking for some objective truth about whether or not their appearance measured up to some external standard. The phenomenon began to bother Helene more and more. Even asking a seemingly benign question such as "How do you like this style on me?" was to give credibility to one of the beauty myths—the myth that anyone else can tell you how you should look. Helene began to discipline herself not to bring up the question of looks, or engage in the tell-the-truth game with other women. "There's some level of self-acceptance simply in not talking about it," Helene says.

Redefining Beauty for Ourselves

Helene discovered the ultimate truism about beauty: When you feel great about yourself, you project that feeling with a radiance that draws others to you. But there's no one formula for achieving it. It's defined from within, after shaking off stereotypes. It emerges from feeling healthy, relaxed, and at home in your body, but manifests itself in different ways for different women.

Like Helene, Lynn has dyed her hair red since she was in her twenties, not to cover the gray but because her own brown hair never looked right to her. "I always thought it was just a genetic mistake that I was born with brown hair. I'm actually a redhead." Lynn, a strong-willed nonconformist, was following an internal cue when she decided to change her appearance, not some external idea of how she should look.

It's the difference between choosing clothes because they happen to be "in" and picking out something that looks and feels right. It's just as tyrannical for someone to campaign that women should *never* change their natural appearance as it is for the beauty industry to declare that women should *always* be striving for perfection. There's a balance, which involves no small amount of ambiguity, as women try to sort out what they're doing for themselves versus what they're doing for others. We can give up being slaves to the cosmetic industry, but still love looking good.

Ilene, a radiant sixty-six-year-old who has held workshops and counseled women for years on developing inner beauty, insists it doesn't matter what decisions a woman makes about her external appearance as long as she focuses on the internal self that is the source of real beauty. "I believe that if a woman wants to wear makeup or have cosmetic surgery or color her hair or wear three-thousand-dollar suits, that's fine. I don't have any problem with that. Although I'm a feminist, I think it's foolhardy to be intolerant of steps other women want to take to make themselves look a certain way. But I do say it's a hollow victory if you do not attend to the inside."

When you feel great about yourself, you project that feeling with a radiance that draws others to you. But there's no one formula for achieving it.

The New Age of Beauty

Ilene has a mane of white hair, bright eyes, and a manner that draws others to her. She drives a new red sports car, gives seminars on beauty and agelessness, and is writing a book about older women and younger men. She enjoys the company of people of all ages, but typically dates men at least twenty years younger than she is. She's frustrated with the ageism of society and hopes to be part of a revolution. "We've been given literally millions of messages that tell us that aging is a despicable thing. It's ageism that is a horrible thing. But we've all signed up for it. And we can change it. The problem is not the fear of looking old. The problem is that we don't look at our fears. If all of the millions of Baby Boomers would start having this conversation, we could conquer it in a month."

She finds it ironic that ageism perpetuates itself. "It's killing us," she says. Older people often tend to remove themselves from society, losing access to relationships and stimulation that might otherwise keep them young.

She feels it's possible for anyone to achieve what she has achieved: a welcome place in society, beauty that attracts people, and a zest for living that knows no time bounds. "But," she cautions, "you have to work at it." Ilene swims three times a week, walks every day, takes classes, reads a lot, and socializes with people of all ages. She eats well, avoids alcohol and tobacco, and practices mindful living. "I feel like I'm meditating all the time."

She's an optimist who enjoys people and never stays depressed for long. Taking care of the spirit, she says, is just as important to beauty as taking care of the body. "It helps to make peace with yourself and others, and to stop comparing yourself with other women." Competitiveness breeds resentment and anger and that is the real threat to beauty, she says.

Ilene believes that striving for the media's vision of beauty is actually an impediment because it puts women in impossible situations that leave them feeling frustrated. "Frustration creates the wrong kind of wrinkles." She urges women to come to terms with the inevitability of aging. "We have to accept the reality that a woman's body will change. Our hips spread, our spine compresses, our eyebrows thin and just about disappear. Our lips get thin. Why? Because they do. That's got to be okay. One in two-hundred-thousand women won't have their bodies change, and that's usually because they spend four hours a day in a gym. Who can do that? You can use skin moisturizer, but you have to accept your changes."

According to Ilene, acceptance creates the kind of relaxation and openness that allows a woman's inner beauty to emerge.

> People tell me that I have the light around me. It's all about love. It's being in the present. Not being addicted to what others think. You have to forgive others. You have to learn to use your goodness. You have to have intimacy in your life. We all need closeness. You have to be willing to be beautiful. You have to be willing to be sexy. You have to step outside yourself. Why would a young man want to sleep with a sixty-six-year-old woman who looks her age? Why not. I can't wait for the day when women everywhere begin to say their ages out loud.

Here are a few beauty tips from Ilene: "Take classes in subjects you know nothing about. Become open to friends of different ages, different backgrounds, and different cultures. Forgive old resentments. Celebrate the success of others. Keep learning and growing. And," she says with a grin, "buy a red nightgown."

5

WHEN THE SWEET
YOUNG THING RIPENS

Letting Go of Aging Angst
and Reinventing What Is Hip

The great thing about getting older is that you don't lose all the other ages you've been.

—Madeleine L'Engle

Age is something that doesn't matter unless you are a cheese.

—Billie Burke

When I was young, I was frightened I might bore other people, now I am old I am frightened they will bore me.

—Ruth Adam

Summer of Love

In terms of living youth to the fullest, Salli's timing couldn't have been better. She was young and free and hip during the sixties and seventies. Plus, she lived in the epicenter of the youth revolution, San Francisco's Haight-Ashbury. "You could walk down the street barefoot, in your flowing dress, and tourists would look at you like you were weird. And you'd feel a little sad, because they couldn't be like you." She grins. "And you'd also feel a little cool, because they couldn't be like you." Salli was young when youth suddenly began to stand for power, energy, sex, beauty, and revolutionary ideas. It also became a scary time when drugs and disenchantment moved in, and people got arrested and beat up for expressing some of these wild new thoughts.

She tells luscious stories about Janis Joplin sleeping in her living room and Joan Baez raising her political consciousness. When Salli says, "I was there for it all," you know she feels lucky to have been young in the sixties. But what you notice more about Salli is that she isn't stuck in her wild, young past.

She seems just as ecstatic to be fifty-something at the end of the nineties. She hasn't missed a beat. She's moving right along with the culture, in some instances pushing ahead of it. For Salli, the goal is not to recapture youth, because she embodies the essential parts of it—curiosity, vitality, eagerness to learn, willingness to experiment. She says the task is to remain relevant. "Fear of aging is about fear of social death, of being invisible."

Time moves on, and so does Salli. While others try to deny or beat back age, Salli demonstrates that you don't have to be chronologically young to be hip. Picture Salli today, on her hillside overlooking a wide valley, tending to her garden in the early morning, in long gauzy dress and Birkenstocks, weathered straw hat over wispy blonde hair with a wild purple streak down the back.

She even plays with the taboo subject of death as she shows off her "Coffin Garden"—small, raised flowerbeds whose wooden frames are in the unmistakable six-sided shape of a coffin. One flower plot with apple and persimmon trees and a wooden totem is for her friend, folksinger Kate Wolf, who died in her forties of leukemia. Kate's song "Redtail Hawk," celebrating "the golden, rolling hills of California," had to have been inspired by a view similar to Salli's. She also has two raised beds of California poppies and cornflowers as pre-planted memorials for herself and her husband.

This unusual garden plot is in keeping with Salli's current interest—the changing rituals about death and dying—a subject she has embraced with typical enthusiasm and is incorporating into a book. She is not alone in this, but again she is part of the leading edge of a trend—to make peace with death by talking about it instead of trying to deny it. "I want to introduce new rituals that bring us together, to celebrate life and acknowledge someone's passing. Clearly we have to have lots of conversations about death so we can fully understand, as much as possible, what it means to die. The universe seems to be calling me to pay attention to death. It feels right to focus on this topic now so I will have a good death and the best life possible." Salli's current work in progress, *Death: The Last Dance,* largely on ritual and conversations about death, is her seventh book. The first was on how to start a free school, a recent one was about staying true to your creative self. In between, there were books on dealing with money and marketing. All motivated, she says, by what interested her personally at the time. "Writing is my window into the world, the way I find out how the world works."

Friends say of Salli that she is constantly reinventing herself. What she's kept all along, no matter which milestone birthday she marks, is delight, energy, and imagination. People pay attention to Salli's presence in the room. She's a sunny magnet, to all ages.

"I decided a long time ago that I want to always stay connected with the period that is now." says Salli. "I want to feel it in my pores. I don't want to be twenty-one again or thirty. But I want the connection with those who are. It's energizing. I want to keep abreast of the culture, not by watching TV or reading newspapers but by staying in touch with people. I want to communicate with younger people, and not just with me telling the stories. I want to hear about my goddaughter's life at Bryn Mawr. Really feel how it is to live that. I want my connections to be a two-way thing."

Salli doesn't want to be simply the wise woman speaking from on high, she wants to be in the middle of things. "I remember, when I first moved from the city to the country, sitting at the feet of the old Italian farmers." (She hoots as she says, "Those same farmers were probably only ten years older than I am now.") "They knew so much. Where to get seed. How to plant potatoes. And I would study them and listen. . . . I like that part as I get older—being a teacher. But it's easy to fall into *just* being a teacher. I also love it when I go to a party and a nine-year-old runs over and gives me a big hug or grabs my hand and we go for a skip."

Meanwhile, Back at the Mirror

Even the ever-evolving Salli admits that she's thought about lying about the numbers—but in a direction that few women could imagine. "Once I thought maybe I should actually say I was older than I am so that people would always say, 'Wow, you look so much younger.' But I think I should have started that a few years back. When I look at photos of me from ten years ago, I think I was cool looking. I like the way I look today but it surprises me that those same pictures are ones that at the time I didn't think were very flattering." Salli's reaction to old pictures sounds familiar.

Barbara, looking forward to her thirty-year high school re-union, says, "I look at old photos and wonder why I was so worried about my hips and my stomach back then. I looked terrific." Given a choice, how many women would rather look younger than they are or actually be younger? The growing popularity of so-called age-defying cosmetics would suggest an overwhelming vote for erasing the visible signs of aging. So, is it that we want to look young or be young?

Kim says, "If someone told me I could shave off a year or two, I can't think of any actual year I'd be willing to sacrifice. That means giving up years that had your kids' birthday parties or a fabulous sunset or at least one good dinner out. I don't want to lose the years I've had. The little lines around my mouth. That's something different."

Grace, a beautician and artist, spends a lot of her time at work in front of a mirror. "I had a dream at age thirty-five that I looked into a mirror and saw an old woman. It scared me and

I drew back and said, "How did this happen?" The old woman said, "You're not paying attention." I knew I was telling myself to get real and face it.... What makes me mad is that women feel like we've done something bad by growing older."

Barbara got aging angst from her mother. "She was always beautiful, and that has been important to her. She is the most loving and nonjudgmental person, except about looks. The other day she said she didn't know how Barbra Streisand could get such a good-looking man. And I said, 'What about the fact that she's brilliant and talented and powerful?'"

I look forward to the time when I can
stop obsessing about looking young. I
actually worry about how much I'm caught
up now in being the cute young thing.

Boomer Panic

The older woman has become sought after by cosmetic manufacturers, who stay up nights thinking about her, scheming ways to get her attention. Unfortunately it is her insecurity about aging that they find so attractive. There's a huge and growing market in the panicky Baby Boomer. Forty-one percent of cosmetic surgeries are done on thirty-five- to fifty-year-olds (women *and* men). One-third of American women surveyed said they buy anti-aging creams and moisturizers. That women worry about looking older as they grow older is no big news flash, and Boomers are hardly the first generation to bet money on youth in a jar. Remember the lotions on your mother's vanity? Her lanolin was our version of collagen cream, Retin-A, and alpha hydroxy. Still, the lure that something is going to make us look twenty-five again merely underscores the message that older ages are unattractive. Shea, at age thirty-six, says, "I look forward to the time when I can stop obsessing about looking young. I actually worry about how much I'm caught up now in being the cute young thing. I need to shift away from it. I look forward to giving it up and being who I am."

For Shea, the messages against aging don't come from Mom, but from Dad. Her father is sixty years old, but he looks fifty and is driven to stay young. "It's rubbed off on me." A mother of three and a teacher's aide, Shea gets up every morning at 6 A.M. to run. Shea is hopeful the Baby Boomer generation may change some of that obsession. "I think it's starting to happen," she observes, mentioning how satisfying it felt to see actress Diane Keaton, now in her fifties, actually play a woman in her fifties.

Certainly, the generation that has affected so much of the culture has the numbers and clout to also tweak the image of aging. With many Boomers already hitting fifty, there's a large vested interest in making that milestone more a positive than a negative. It's ironic too that while technology is helping us live longer, the culture continues to send the message that it's best to be young. "So big deal, you can live to one hundred," says Jane. "But you don't want anyone to think you look it. And you don't dare tell anyone you're getting close."

"You know," says Barbara, "technically, we're young for only a short time, compared to how long we're old. I realized recently that this is the body I'm going to have for a long time. I better take care of it."

One thing women can do is refuse to be part of ageism, because it will only end up sabotaging them. Don't laugh at little-old-lady jokes and ignore those ads like the one for the moisturizer that says, "See your mother on holidays. Not every time you look in the mirror." Rather than denying that aging will ever happen to them, some women are collecting role models so they'll be ready. "I think I want to be zany when I'm old," Neva says. "I was at a wedding where a ninety-year-old woman stood up at the reception, sang a love song, and danced the hula. She was tall and proud and she had a look on her that told us she was just showing us who she was. It was part madness and part delight. Everyone applauded."

Oh, Grow Up!

Salli says, "I know that I'm growing older but I don't understand the people who groan, 'Oh god, I'm going to be forty-five.' I don't go the other way either. I don't read crone books. I don't join crone circles. I hate the word *crone*." Yet, Salli doesn't spend a lot of time on physical maintenance. "I don't invest as much as my friends do. I don't go to spas. If I don't get exercise by walking or working in the garden, I don't get it at all. Fear of flab and wrinkles is something that doesn't come up much in my world. Concern over aches and pains and loss of agility does."

Barbara says, "I lie in bed at night and think of the things I should do. Like diet and go to the gym. But then when I'm up, I'd rather be working in my backyard. Then the other day I was out getting my mail, and this guy drove by me and he didn't even look. It was like I wasn't even there. I still want heads to turn."

Justine, a lawyer and single mother, says, "I've noticed lately that men don't look at me like the way they used to."

Jane adds, "The first time I went to the fair and saw the carnival guys ogling my teenage daughter I was furious. How dare they look at her that way. But part of me was wondering why they weren't looking at me that way. I wouldn't admit that in most feminist circles."

Salli is ten years older than her husband. "I think of him as my age. If he were with a younger woman would he do different things? Maybe. But he likes being with me. Sometimes I'll overhear him talking about me. He says I'm really upbeat. He says I keep him going. We are not an age match; we are a personality match." At the same time she says he keeps her young. "He encourages the little girl part of me. I can be a kid around him. I'm afraid of heights but he held my hand and helped me climb a Mayan pyramid." Part of Salli's energy force comes from her sense of adventure.

> I do scary things all the time. I'm not a great swimmer, but on our vacation I swam out to a reef because that's where the best snorkeling was. I'm nervous about audiences, but I go on TV and I give speeches in front of two hundred people. Someday I might stop trying new things, and then you can ask me and I'll say I guess I feel older. But even when I'm eighty I'll have a lot of costumes and will change my clothes several times a day. I will probably be a bit wacky, but pleasantly so. I hear that older people take naps. I don't take naps.

Lost and Found Pleasures

For some women, age brings freedom to go back to the things we loved so much when we were young—or to start something new. We're not as self-conscious anymore, we know we don't have to be perfect, and we can indulge in activities just for the fun of it.

After years of dreaming about having her own pleasure boat, Jeannie has scored a small aluminum skiff with a motor and little canopy in which to roam the backwaters of a nearby lake. She wanted something that gets her to a swimming hole, away from the jet skis and private enough to go skinny dipping. She gets more, however, than swimming unencumbered. She finds solitude and quiet. A different focus. Time out, by herself. Dream time.

Gretchen, a teacher, returned to playing the cello after a twenty-year absence. On mornings when school's out, she sits, with a cup of coffee beside her, in her living room playing her cello. Her sons are away, living on their own. Her husband leaves for work early. The house is hers. Only the cats are around to hear. "I love it." She purrs. "It's the best thing I do for myself. It makes me happy. I'm never packing my cello away again. I always told the kids, one day I'd start playing again. But there wasn't time in my thirties."

For others it's horseback riding or painting, or starting something new like improvisational acting. Diana, a health professional, took up acting. "I decided I needed to make a right angle in my life." Could it be there's a trend here, to schedule room in our overbooked lives for a passion? To pursue something for the simple private pleasure of it? Mark that down as one advantage of getting older—taking the time to renew an old love or find a new one. When Diana walks out on stage, her face lights up with the excitement of a twelve-year-old. Then there's the mom who is learning to be a stand-up comic. And the hairdresser who's trying her hand at poetry. What a great birthday present—lost and found pleasures. Think back to what's on hold. Imagine the possibilities.

"My family expected me to be traditional," says Salli, who grew up in Ohio. "Get ahead and get a Buick. I love my family, but I felt like I was different and there wasn't a lot of support for being creative." She was nineteen when she and her musician-husband took off for San Francisco. "We didn't read about it in the paper and say let's go. It was really before everyone started migrating there. We just knew we didn't want to be in Ohio. For some reason the people who came to San Francisco felt we were from the same planet." Today she still hasn't figured out what the lure was. "It makes you believe in synchronicity. It was a big, extended family with real love and openness. We were innocent. Under the velvet dresses and hippie beads there was real sharing. We'd get on motorcycles and drive through Golden Gate Park at night with the lights off. But we weren't the people who had a mattress on the floor and multiple sex partners."

She was right in the middle of it all. Her husband at the time organized the Quicksilver Messenger Service band. But then drugs moved into the Haight, and Salli moved to another part of the city and helped found an unstructured private school, known back then as a "free school." Friends got clubbed and teargassed by the police at San Francisco State University for having the wrong politics. She got a divorce and she and her daughter moved again to a small northern California town where Salli helped start another school and wrote a book about it.

Was she aware that she was in the middle of a social transformation? "Well, you wore the clothes. You were outrageous. You were thinking, 'Ha, ha, Cincinnati.' We didn't have much responsibility, but we took care of each other. We had time to talk for hours. None of it was planned."

She kept finding herself at the forefront of social change. She lived on a commune in the country, spun wool, and crocheted hats. She taught dream workshops and tie dye, as well as a class on "man and nature" at the local university. She changed her last name to Rasberry—dropping the "p" to make it her own. "It's my favorite fruit, favorite color and it's luscious." For a while she even dropped Salli, going only by Rasberry. When she turned thirty she remembers saying, "I'm getting older. I'd better do something with my life." That's when she started writing. "Suddenly I had a career." It was the last time she recalls worrying about being a certain age. She knows, however, that others worry.

"I don't mind being my age," she says, smirking. "But I don't like that being over fifty labels me. A young guy at the store called me 'lady' and I thought 'ick.' He's nineteen. I don't want to be nineteen, but I don't want his age and my age to be barriers to each other. I also don't like it when people call older women 'girls.' We're not girls. They think they're being nice. But they're being patronizing."

Ask Salli how she would be today if she hadn't moved to San Francisco and she immediately hunches over and makes a pained face. "I'd have developed some frailty so I could get attention. I'd be in the DAR and wearing pantyhose. Oh god."

Making Priorities

Salli began writing about creativity as she hit middle age. She thought it important to do so at this point. "Once you're a certain age, you don't want to feel stuck and stifled and then just cruise out for the next thirty years. Every book I've written is so I can understand things better. I always felt it was important to grow and change all the time, but keep the center. My priorities have always been to cherish my family and friendships and grow my garden. They all need nourishment."

In recent years she added caring for her grandchildren and staying healthy to her top concerns. She doesn't worry about her looks changing, but she has some concern about her body parts functioning the way they used to. Recently she had some problems with her knees. "That scared me. I always liked old people and felt bad when I saw that some of them couldn't jump. You know, just leap or hop off a step. When my knees started hurting I thought, 'Oh no, what if I can't jump?'"

The Tough Parts

Worries about aging go way beyond vanity and some discomfort when the talk moves from aging angst to dread of becoming sick and infirm.

"There are more things to worry about with aging than not having a flat stomach," says Natalie, who suddenly, at age forty, is caring for her seriously ill parents. "I used to mind that my back is starting to hurt when I jog, but I'm learning that's nothing."

"Our fear of aging," Jeannie offers, "is really about the simple fear of dying. I remember hearing someone say how amazing it is to live in a society where we witness death all around us and still believe as individuals that it won't happen to us."

Barbara says, "Maybe fear of the physical part of aging is merely a distraction. This fear of flab keeps us busy." She laughs and then turns serious as she recalls her breast cancer scare. "I realized I was worried about losing a breast or having a lumpec-tomy or radiation and getting hard breasts. I concentrated on how I would look, so I didn't have to face the real fear, that my daugh-ters might lose their mother ... That I could die."

Maybe fear about the physical part
of aging is merely a distraction.
This fear of flab keeps us busy.

Now for the Role Models

Salli has women to whom she looks for cues on aging. One is her mother-in-law. "Capable, steady, and independent. She is a master photographer who travels the world. Until recently she did her own darkroom work and now, in her eighties, has taught herself to use a computer and is scanning her photos and enhancing them on it. She doesn't whine about getting older and neither does she glorify it."

Another role model for Salli is a social activist also in her eighties. Salli calls her "one of the sexiest women I have ever met. Being sexy has a lot to do with energy and I can't really explain it but she has 'it' in abundance. She has style and flair. She is both sure of herself and vulnerable. She has tons of friends and loves a good party." Tina Turner is one of her famous role mod-els—"Pure energy, bigger than life, non-stop boogie. She's gutsy. When I think I can't do something, I think of Tina Turner and I know I can."

And how does Salli think her old pal Janis Joplin might have aged had she lived?

"If she were still here, Janis Joplin would be singing in a gospel choir. She would have the largest collection of capes in the world. She would be married and her friends would gather in her home to make music. She would take long walks on the beach, and her fans would leave her alone. She would be grounded and adventurous ... yet not quite content."

6

Breaking Out of the Good Old Boys' Network

Letting Go of the Old Work Rules and Bringing More of Yourself to the Job

Unfortunately, there are still many women in the business world who refuse to support women. I call them "Honorary Males"—women who think that power is to be had only in the company of men. Women must realize they have power—economic and political. Don't give your power away; use it for yourself and for the benefit of other women.

—Ginger Purdy

Success can make you go one of two ways. It can make you a primadonna—or it can smooth the edges, take away the insecurities, let the nice things come out.

—Barbara Walters

Out of the Loop

She doesn't know for sure if it's a basic male/female difference or if it's just a matter of personal style, but Darla knows she looks at the world differently than many of the men in her life. "When we're skiing, my husband wants to conquer the mountain, while I'm more interested in seeing the scenery and going down the mountain with some style," she says with a laugh. The two world views can be reconciled easily enough on a weekend ski trip. Regardless of what's on their minds when they set off down the mountain, afterwards Darla and her husband end up agreeably cozy together in the lodge with hot drinks in their hands.

But, when it comes to the workplace, it hasn't always been easy for Darla to reconcile the yin and the yang. When she got a new job as a middle manager in a computer graphics firm, Darla struggled through an uphill climb to gain respect from the men at the top. She enjoys a collaborative work style, focusing on people and process rather than forced productivity. Her style looked soft to fellow managers. They wanted her to get tough. But Darla just couldn't get behind the "because-I'm-the-boss-that's-why" approach. Instead, if one of her employees was grumbling, she'd suggest time out for coffee and find out why. Sure it slowed production for a while, but the investment of fifteen minutes for listening and two dollars for a latte would pay off later when her workers felt they'd been heard. "I'd like to think that the heart of my management style is giving people opportunity, and not imposing control. A manager is like an agent, giving other people a chance to succeed. The person being managed knows you've got their best interest at heart. It's not entirely unselfish. If that person succeeds, it's a feather in your cap."

When Darla first arrived on the job, she listened politely to other managers' opinions about her department, and nodded at the rundown on the reputations of various employees. Then she cleared her head and resolved to take a hands-off approach until she could develop her own point of view. She refused to jump right in with directives to her employees. Nor would she chime in with other managers' put-downs of certain workers. Pretty soon she was out of the loop with those at the top of the corporate structure, and her own job appeared to be teetering on the line.

Her Way

For decades, women have been making progress in gaining equal access to the corporate world. Looking at the number of women who are in management and own businesses, it would appear that we're moving in on the goal. It was not that long ago that the most acceptable career goals for women were nurse or teacher. The Baby Boomer generation helped make a turnabout. Today there are opportunities in almost every profession for women.

But there's still the glass ceiling. In many organizations, women are having trouble getting past a certain point. Especially in businesses where there's a long history of control-based management styles, some women feel like a fish out of water, unable to exercise their natural method for getting from point A to point B because there's not enough oxygen in the room to do anything more than try to survive.

Women often enjoy a more collaborative approach to work. There's a pride in companionability, with interpersonal issues weighing in heavily alongside professional goals. It probably wasn't a woman who first used "that's business" as an excuse for exercising cutthroat tactics to get ahead. Not that women always get along—we've all heard the horror stories—but more often than not, there's a desire for quality relationships as well as getting the job done.

When women get into situations where their instincts don't seem to be working for them, sometimes they give up and play by the old rules—making blatant power plays or manipulating their way around co-workers. Others try to rise above the competitive fray only to end up accepting a trade-off of less power for more peace of mind. Then there are those who turn to mush, trying so hard to please others that they lose their ability to get things done.

Darla, however, is one of the success stories. She walked through the fire and emerged unscarred, with people cheering. She's an example of someone who drew on her internal resources for cues about how to be effective without losing her soul. These days she can look back and recall the small triumphs that helped her find her way.

One image Darla remembers clearly from her difficult days is how one of her bosses would always start looking at his watch the minute she started to speak. "I know I sometimes ramble when I talk, and that puts people off. I started trying to express myself in as few words as possible, but that didn't seem to work either." Over and over again, she looked for ways to communicate to her bosses what she was doing as a new manager. She was taking time to get to know the strengths of each of her employees and giving them some room to exercise their creativity. She arranged her work schedule to keep her life in balance, and encouraged her employees to do the same. She encouraged risk-free brainstorming sessions and her workers followed suit. It was okay not to have all the answers; answers came with time. Though she was making drastic changes in her department, progress was slow.

Her process wasn't easily explained in corporate speak. One day, her supervisor took her out to lunch for a "corrective interview" about how she did her work. "He hated my approach. He said I was a flake. He thought my style was way out there and odd. He wanted me to work on my behavior."

The message was clear. Other managers wanted her to be more controlling. But that would have required a personality transplant for Darla, not to mention a shift in her fundamental values. So she had to develop some strategies for coping with the disapproval, protecting herself from the sting of criticism, and establishing a rapport with other managers, all while getting the work done. The dilemma was she had the good-girl quality of wanting to be liked. But, she couldn't do the right thing on behalf of her staff without risking the ire of her own bosses.

So, she took a stand. Darla wouldn't join the Old Boys' Network if that meant not supporting her employees. Not only was it anathema to her, she had no idea how to play the game. On the other hand, she did not have the financial option of breaking down and screaming, "I quit!" At the time, she was the main breadwinner in the family, with three young children and a mortgage. She had to stick it out, somehow.

Fortunately, Darla had a track record of success at a previous workplace and a mentor whose past teachings she could call upon in her time of struggle with the new corporation. She took a lot of long walks—"it gets the lactic acid out of my system"—and remembered her mentor's advice to respect and encourage the talents of employees, giving them positive feedback and as much free rein as possible. She knew she could make it work in this corporation as she had done before, and she resolved to get her bosses behind her. Niceness hadn't worked, but integrity would. "I had to speak up," she says, "and I started by asking my boss to stop glancing at his watch every time I talked. That got his attention. He said, 'You know, my wife tells me the same thing.'"

Once she began standing up for herself, Darla was able to open up the lines of communication. Her strategy was to deflect her boss's criticism by getting a clearer idea of what was bothering him and what his goals were. It was the same tactic she'd used with her employees. Ultimately, she forged an alliance by making an effort to understand him.

> I've tried to teach myself and other women that if you can help your supervisors feel more comfortable, they will trust you. Sometimes they're more afraid than you are. I set about to make my supervisors feel safer with me. Rather than waiting for my boss to support me, I supported him in things. There were things he wanted to accomplish, and I could help him.

After she convinced her boss that she understood and shared his goals, he backed off from meddling with her department. Then, when he saw how smoothly everything was running, he relaxed in his criticism.

Soon her department was producing some innovative work and receiving high praise from outside the company. Then the awards started coming in. The man who had once called her a "flake" was now advising other managers to follow Darla's lead. Eventually many of her techniques became *de rigeur* in other departments, as a more worker-centered, team-based approach was instituted.

When Darla announced that she was moving to a different state—for both career and family reasons—people at all levels of the company were disappointed. Her employees say she's pretty much adored by everyone, even by those who weren't entirely happy with her decisions. She wasn't perfect, they say, but she was always accessible—someone who makes a genuine connection and uses it to work together toward common goals. "At some point, we started calling her a goddess," says one artist who worked under Darla. One day, after she'd moved, the workers in her department joined together in a mock group wail that echoed through the office. Another artist explained, "Every once in a while we have to cry together over losing her."

Who Do You Think You Are?

Conflict, criticism, and struggle are routine forms of hazing for most people who achieve success in the workplace. But there are plenty of women who simply do not want to enter the arena. They may have great ideas and the potential to be visionary leaders, but something in them shrinks from the prospect of putting themselves out there. Maybe they are the same ones who, years ago, couldn't stand the way boys reacted when they asked for a turn in tetherball. When they asked to play the game, they put themselves on the line and were open to criticism. The women who make it through the hazing are usually those who have confidence in themselves and others, and somehow can tune out the static long enough to prove their competence.

Women who win political seats, achieve commercial success, or even just use their voices a little loudly in the workplace find themselves taking flak for it. Often the critics aren't being intentionally sexist, but there's an underlying message of discrimination in the kind of attention successful women get.

Martha Stewart built a financial empire on her expertise in the domestic arts. Instead of being universally praised for her business acumen, she's taken a flood of criticism from people who say she's just not, well, nice. She is said to be a hard-driving boss, outspoken and demanding. If she were a man, she'd be featured regularly on the cover of *Forbes* magazine. Considering the way some critics have gone after Hillary Clinton, some people think that the word "pillory"—as in public ridicule—should be changed to "Hillary." What happened to the outspoken first lady was a warning to other women.

One thing we can all do is analyze our criticism of women in power—whether it's our boss, someone on the town council, or a superstar—and ask if we'd have the same criticism of a man. How many times are women put down as "too fluffy," "bitchy," "hard," "dumb," or, in Darla's case, "flaky"?

Women who win political seats, achieve commercial success, or even just use their voices a little loudly in the workplace find themselves taking flak for it.

At work, it helps when women begin talking to one another and acknowledge that, often, there are gender-related issues that come up in the workplace—an admission that was spoken only in whispers a couple of decades ago, when the goal of equality meant that you simply did not emphasize the difference between men and women. When women get together, some common observations bubble up about the atmosphere as they reach higher levels of management. Once we admit the issues exist, then we can get past them.

Women at Work

When women talk about their work experience in gender terms, there's no general consensus about a definitive woman's style. What they seem to share, however, is the view that there are alternatives to the classically male model of doing business. There are professions where the collaborative approach is thriving among women, and workplaces where changes reflect a growing acceptance that business should adapt to real life rather than the other way around.

Rhonda, a nurse:
I work in a medical clinic with mostly women. We really care about each other and it's not like we're faking it. We don't talk behind each other's backs because we can say it to each other. If someone makes a mistake, we talk about it. 'This happened and how can you make it better?' We know we're all human and communication is critical. When we hire people, one of our criteria is that they're good people. When people separate their work from their lives, what do they have left? What are we spending most of our lives doing?

Lynn, an architect:
Architects tend to do designs "for" people, but I take a collaborative approach, asking clients to participate in the process as much as possible so the final result is more functional for them. At first, my male colleagues thought my approach was strange, but now it's more common in the profession.

Justine, an attorney:
I work in an office with all women. Before, I had to compete with the men I worked with because that's how they do it. That's their natural way of doing it. With women, I can't say it's necessarily entirely cooperative. Everyone has their different purposes. Some are more businesslike, some are more idealistic. There are still the conflicts. But it's not the competitive thing it was in an office with all men.

Jane, a writer:
It was an eye-opener in our office when a few men in management got divorced at around the same time and arranged shared custody with their ex-wives. Suddenly, it was acceptable to rush out to pick up your child after school, or to be late because you had a parent/teacher conference in the morning. Our union contract even changed to allow us to take sick days when we need to stay home with an ill child. Men finally understood what it meant to balance home and career, something working mothers have been juggling for years.

So, yes, there have been improvements. But, as Darla learned, there's still a wide gap between the concept of equality and the reality of what it means to earn success—your way—in businesses and professions that were predominantly male territory until fairly recently. Your goals may be lofty, but to achieve the greater good may mean some bouts with what feels like bad-girl behavior.

Justine has discovered that to be successful in the legal arena, sometimes she has to play hard ball. But she is hopeful that women are having more influence.

I'm a lawyer, and that has been a male-dominated arena. . . . I think it's kind of claw-and-manipulate until you get to the place where you know your value, where you know you have the experience, and you have the confidence to say, "This is what I think, this is what's going to happen, and this is why." When you align women who can still hold on to their caring ways with men who are also compassionate . . . then that combination changes the world. You still have to be tough and sometimes you have to be an asshole and you have to just say, "This is what's happening because it's right. I don't care if you like it or not. There it is." It's hard because I know I have to resist wanting that person to still like me, especially if they're opposing counsel.

Barbara, who has a bookkeeping business:
I learned a lot from playing sports that seems to apply to the work world. To win in tennis I have to somehow unconsciously alienate myself from my opponent. I have to make them my enemy in order to slam the ball and to really play my hardest. I have to separate wanting to win from wanting to be liked.

Joy, former business owner:
There is a way that wanting to get along and wanting to make nice gets in the way of being able to do your work. It takes a certain amount of mental energy . . . and submission. If you're submitting, chances are you're not really performing.

One recurring theme in conversations with successful women is their awareness of how women tend to take things more personally—and how others can use that to manipulate them. Patty, a college administrator known for her savvy in political matters, was shaken when a one-time friend twisted information about her into a vicious rumor designed to undermine Patty's credibiity. Patty had always believed in fair play, and even though she'd faced problems, she believed "people generally are trying to do their best in life." Her husband gave her a reality check, advising that her optimism left her vulnerable. These days, she has her antennae up for unscrupulous types, and is careful to keep her personal life and opinions protected from them.

Women who have survived personal attacks often emerge with better defenses, making sure they aren't vulnerable to the jab that aims for the heart. Detachment, some say, is the way to survive. But seasoned observers say that it doesn't seem to come as naturally for women as for men.

Jessica, a political leader and project manger, has observed distinct gender styles. She doesn't encourage following the male example but believes there's power in being aware of how the good old boys operate. "Men are better at cutting backroom deals than women. Politics and business are like playing a game, and men are very good at joking around and making everyone feel at ease while they shrewdly wheel and deal. They make it look easy and try to put people at ease. Often when women are running the meeting or the business, they seem a bit stiff and 'professional' and the whole persona does not seem to come naturally."

Jessica thinks women often take things much more personally than men, especially when there is a difference of opinion.

> Many successful women I work with who have served in public office were very responsible, controlling, oldest-children-in-the-family types. They seem to take things very seriously and they make the work look difficult and stressful.
>
> The biggest difference between men and women for me, though, has been that many women truly care if they've voted against a woman colleague they consider a friend, or if they've fired or reprimanded a co-worker. For men, it seems to be part of the game—vote and forget about it, fire the folks and forget about it.

Natalie, a scriptwriter:
Men don't obsess over their work relationships the way women do. My husband is like that and he is not a macho kind of guy at all. He doesn't do sports, he doesn't do hi-fives, he's not a back-slapper, he's not a joiner. But he still doesn't obsess over how to get things done. He just does it and says, "I don't give a damn what other people say." It just doesn't occur to him. He doesn't understand why I'm concerned about what others think of my work. He says, "Why do you care? Why don't you just do it?" It just always seems easier for him in the workplace. Probably because the bosses are men.

Justine:
I don't think men think as hard about this stuff as we do.

Jeannie, a business owner:
The average man works. That's what he does. He works. He probably doesn't have a couple of kids to cook dinner for. He's probably more relaxed or feeling less responsible for cleaning his house. He probably has a woman who takes care of him. Of the men who are in my office, there's one who is a part-time parent, but everyone else has a female mate who is there on a day-to-day basis to support him.

Work as Dysfunctional Family

Women who struggle with relationships at work often analyze the problems in familial terms. Many characterize a troubled workplace as a "dysfunctional family" and draw parallels between work relationships and family roles.

Kim, a stockbroker:
Management is very much like being a parent. I'm not sure there is so much difference between men and women. I see the biggest difference between secure, competent people versus insecure, incompetent people. Insecure managers are very controlling where secure managers give their employees freedom and a feeling of self-worth.

Mary, a legal services attorney:
My boss is very nice and that seems to be the problem. I think that this is a common problem with women bosses—I know I do this, too. She deflects my anger. I will go in determined to have it out with her about something . . . and she'll just say, "It's my fault." She will then go on to be just so nice that I can't continue to bitch at her, so I feel vaguely angry all the time. . . . I regret to say that I have never had trouble with male bosses but have a lot of trouble with women. I think this has to do with my mother problems. I resent older women telling me what to do. It's helpful to consciously separate the boss from your mother.

Shea, a teacher's aide:
I think there are some parallels between how we see our

male bosses and how we saw Dad running the show and saying, "This is how we're going to go on our trip." Even though I don't work in a business dominated by men—I work in the schools—talking to men in administration reminds me of turning to the father and letting him set the tone. But then I'm overly connected to my father in a way I don't like. It's wonderful to grow out of that and be able to be around him and not really care what he thinks either way. I do speak up, and do say what I want, but it's very hard work. I have to prep myself and be on edge. If I anticipate a situation where he'd be guiding me or saying what I should do, I get ready to use my voice. I'm learning to do that at work, too.

Jane:

It's true—in some ways, going to your boss is like dealing with your dad or your boyfriend. It's such a male/female thing. It's like, "Okay, how am I going to do this? Am I going to be rejected? Who cares if I'm rejected? I care if I'm rejected."

Natalie:

I can take care of my sister or my colleague, but not myself, in the workplace. When I work in an office I can go to the boss and say, "You are treating that person unfairly. You can't do that. Here are the rules." But I can't do it for myself. I go in there and I just dissolve. It's pretty hard to stand up to the person who, whether it's your father in real life or your father in the workplace, is supposed to be the guy who leads you along and supports you and shows you how to do things. But over the years you get older, in your life and in the workplace. And you find out that man is not perfect.

I like the team-based management approach where you flatten the top and bring it down, that's a cooperative thing. It's people working together. In my ideal workplace there are men, but people know how to work together. Then when things don't work, we all take responsibility instead of blaming someone. It's not that man at the top who's supposed to be perfect. Together we look at a project that didn't work and figure out how we might do it better.

Don't Take It Personally

Some women are helped by detaching from their relationships at work. It's a relief to give up the goal of being liked. The real strength seems to emerge when women feel free to choose, making real alliances with like-minded colleagues, giving up the illusion that it's possible to be liked by everyone.

Justine:
The nice thing about law is it's not your fight. You're helping with someone else's fight. So I can be up against another lawyer and then see them at a party and really like them. I might not like them in the court setting, but that doesn't necessarily continue outside court. As I do it more and more, I get better at it.

Jane:
I guess women are at the point where we're still trying to figure out the strategy. In a male-run operation, men don't have to figure out how to do it. I think they know. They go out and drink with each other, maybe they talk with each other at the urinal. I don't know what all goes on, but they just kind of know. The pattern is there for them.

But I think women may have an advantage because we're more conscious of how we're working with each other. We're more aware because there are no prescribed ways for women in business to act.

I've often gotten my way at work by being the nice person, very agreeable, the accommodating person, but one day I was furious about something and decided to go into my boss's office and not smile for the entire time. That is hard for me because I smile all the time. Every time this manager would look at me like it was my turn to smile and say, "Oh well, I understand," I didn't. I really had to steel myself and not smile. I'd like to report I got everything I wanted. I didn't. But I felt a hell of a lot better when I walked out of there. I didn't feel like I compromised myself and I made a very strong point. I think I really confused him.

Lynn, an architect:
I've learned not to wait for someone to grant me permission.

Barbara:
There's a difference between being totally fake and being nice.

Is It Worth It?

Making a conscious effort to manage one's behavior, learn the strategy, and play the game carries a high price, says Jessica, who has traveled the world and dealt with leaders in business and politics. She says she has seen women figure out the Old Boys' Network and play by those rules, losing themselves in the process.

A woman can get into the Old Boys' Network. This is done by playing a very specific game with clear rules. The woman is cool, calm, and collected. She listens very carefully and makes very intelligent, useful comments at strategic times during discussions. The woman is very serious and takes on responsibility little by little and does not seem to be a threat. She is not secretary-type useful, but she is an asset because she shows that she can handle difficult situations and smooth things over for the dysfunctional boss or not-so-intelligent political body she serves on. This woman volunteers to clean up the finances, write the proposals, run the central and regional offices, supervise the staff, and she works all the time. Her hair is perfect and her clothes are simple and classy and she always looks well groomed, in control, and never flashy. . . . Little by little the woman learns to wheel and deal and cut backroom deals. She is a team player. She is never a loose cannon and never steps out of her role as a competent, capable, innovative, intelligent person who can always be counted on to fix the messes and cover up the weird behavior of the boss or other director in the firm or the organization.

What happens to the woman is that she becomes dead to her feelings. She has problems with relationships,

she is tense and stressed, and she may have early menopause or eating disorders. Many times she cannot tell
you what she likes to eat or drink or what her passion
in life is because she has spent so much time second-
guessing the wishes of others. She is confused about why
she is not fulfilled when she has the MBA and the job
and the money and the power—and her life is empty.
She has become a man-woman, and the competition and
striving to be perfect eats her up.

Jessica's picture of the "woman who plays the game is pretty
bleak, so let's end this chapter with a picture of Darla, who is no
doubt, at this very moment, behaving like, well, Darla—flounder-
ing around for words to capture a complicated thought, saying,
"Please, just stay with me for a minute . . ." Sending out an in-
teroffice memo about taking a few hours off to go to a function
at her children's school, or sneaking off to a matinee with a few
other exhausted colleagues. Working on a Saturday morning to
catch up in the quiet off-hours. Making a faux pas in a manager's
meeting. Praising the work of a known troublemaker or pitching
an idea from far out in left field. Maybe she's accepting another
one of those awards that keep coming her way. In some people's
eyes, Darla may not come across as the corporate ideal, but she's
succeeding in her own way . . . and a lot of people are watching.

7

WARMING UP TO THE SPOTLIGHT

Letting Go of the Back-Row Seat and Taking Center Stage

Everyone thought I was bold and fearless and even arrogant, but inside I was always quaking.

—Katharine Hepburn

When we have the courage to speak out—to break our silence—we inspire the rest of the "moderates" in our communities to speak up and to vote their views.

—Sharon Schuster

Stage Fright

Can you still hear the voices saying, "You're not going out dressed like that are you? What will people think? Who do you think you are?"

"That was my whole life as a kid," sighs Diana.

Diana grew up to be a private person. She raised three children in a small town in northern California. Gentle and soft spoken, Diana even has a behind-the-scenes job as a dental hygienist. Once the thought of getting up in front of a group of people to talk would have made her hands clammy and her throat dry. That all changed when her daughter was murdered. Everything that once seemed solid was shattered.

When she was finally able to pick up some of the pieces, she found she could not bear to keep them to herself. Her loss led her into the cause of violence against women and she found herself center stage at rallies. And as a way to connect with other women, as well as with a deep part of herself that was now raw and exposed, she began taking acting classes. The stage was a place where she found motivation to continue her life and endure the healing that made her pain bearable.

Women are not required to go through tragedy before they can find their place in the spotlight, but many women are by nature reticent, more comfortable hiding in the chorus than singing a solo. Sometimes it takes a crisis to run a risk of standing out there on her own—and, perhaps, being heard.

Shhh! Somebody
Might Hear You

Taking a break between rehearsals and her new weekly voice lessons, Diana says she has done a lot of thinking about why women resist speaking up—why, for years, she didn't have the courage. She thinks it may go back to the times when expressing contrary opinions could cost your life.

There was a time when each person was celebrated for making their individual contribution. You were born, and people waited to see what your talents were, your gift. Each person was considered necessary. Then they started killing people for their gifts, saying that the devil got into them.

I'll tell you, the first time I stood in the square and spoke out against rape and murder, I felt like I was going to be burned at the stake. For saying what was true but unspeakable.

Out of the Ashes

Diana needed to start speaking out. She wanted to do everything she could to prevent other mothers from suffering the horror she had suffered. She wanted to save other daughters. She was also trying to come to terms with what had happened to her daughter.

Iyan was the oldest of her three children. She had moved to San Francisco, into an apartment, unknowingly, next door to a crack addict. Before the eighteen-year-old with the impish smile had even started art school or begun her urban adventure, a neighbor broke into her apartment to steal a stereo. Maybe Iyan resisted, no one will ever know for sure. But the intruder stabbed her to death. After Iyan's murder, Diana said she had to push on, be strong for her two younger children. "The way to do it was to numb out. You're just in shock for a long time."

Diana made a shrine in her living room, with photos of Iyan, from baby to little girl to teenager with her trademark arched eyebrows. Included was Iyan's teddy bear, a Sesame Street doll, a Mother's Day card. Friends recall the shrine being almost too painful to look at. Iyan's murder made the nightmare come true—the middle-of-the-night, icy dread parents feel when their child is no longer under their roof and they lie there imagining the worst thing that could happen.

Slowly, Diana went public with her grief. She attended every day of the murder trial. The suspect, a thirty-one-year-old man, was sentenced to life imprisonment for first degree murder. During the same period, Diana's friends had begun to explore the issue of violence against women and children. They formed an activist group called Born of Women, which began holding vigils and forming what they called "healing circles" at crime scenes. They went to a jogging trail where a woman was raped, a golf course where a teenager was attacked, a dumpster where a woman's body was found. It was these horrible crimes that led Diana to her voice. "Before that I never spoke. But I finally got that if we felt our grief and spoke of it, maybe then we could stop the violence. We had to make the cries of women heard. It was not just one tragedy, not just my tragedy. If it happened to one of us, it happened to all. My group made a commitment to speak up." The commitment means intervening on the street if they see a woman being harassed or pushed around, at least to ask if she needs help.

It still amazes her that the voice came out of a black and horrible place. "There were times back then when it took courage to just wake up and get out of bed."

> I finally got that if we felt our grief and spoke of it, maybe then we could stop the violence. We had to make the cries of women heard.

Spotlights Don't Always Burn

Her first visits to the stage were motivated by anger and pain, but Diana soon grew comfortable up there. And as the years since her daughter's death passed, she found herself on stage trying out other voices, not just the one in pain. She started to sing and get up in front of people and found she could even be wildly funny.

Diana began enjoying herself again. And, in some ways, that was the most radical thing she had done yet. She'd already broken through the cultural stereotype that says good girls are quiet and keep their opinions, even their grief, to themselves. And no one could blame that voice for hollering out in rage. But now she was challenging a more subtle, insidious social convention. People perceived as victims are expected to somehow fade away, not remain in the public eye. And certainly not smile or laugh or be irreverent.

But Diana's life-changing experience shifted something in her. "Your bubble has been burst, but you still find a 'Here's to Life' place inside you, a reminder to choose to be alive."

Diana began acting in a community theater and became a self-confessed "improv junkie." She says that her performer side is as much a tribute to her daughter as the activist side. "We would be really silly together. Iyan had a zany sense of humor. She wanted to be an artist. It wouldn't have served me or her well to stay small after she died." So Diana is enlarging her repertoire.

She understands now that the stumbling block to performing is generally that "we don't believe in ourselves."

"For a long time my friends have been saying, 'You have such a beautiful voice. You should sing in coffee houses.'" Although she's not ready for coffee houses, she understands now that the stumbling block to performing is generally that "we don't believe in ourselves." Diana has been addressing that issue by taking improvisational acting classes. And it seems to be working. Watch her one night as she is pretending to share a hot-air balloon with a stranger in one of the impromptu scenes thrown at her by her improv teacher. Not only is Diana going on about flying over the Golden Gate Bridge, she is also having to change emotions and faces and voices as fast as her teacher barks the commands out—scared, frustrated, demonic. Friends who remember the quiet Diana are amazed. Diana prefers the word "dazzled." She loves the thrill of dazzling others, but that's not why she does it. "The best part of any of this is when you dazzle yourself—take yourself by surprise by what you can do. There doesn't have to be an audience. It's just the moment. The "Wow" moment, when you feel alive because you've created something. Every one of my dental patients has to hear about improv. I don't give them a choice. I tell them they have to try it. It's so much fun."

For Sandy, who sings professionally, it's not so much about dazzling herself as it is about depending on herself. "Why wouldn't

I trust myself to deliver? I don't let my friends down. I always say to people, 'You can count on me; I'll be there.' So why wouldn't I be there for myself? Of course I won't let me down."

There doesn't have to be an audience. It's just the moment. The "Wow" moment, when you feel alive because you've created something.

Women Applauding Women

In Diana's all-woman improv class, everyone is coaxed into stretching their limits. Pauline, the actor who teaches the group, doesn't allow anyone time to decide if they want to make fools out of themselves or not. Fear of looking like a fool holds people back from the spotlight. In improvisation, there just isn't time for fear. According to Pauline, there are two rules: "You can't say 'No, I can't.' And you can't feel guilty for not doing it right." There is no "right" way in improv, a novel concept for the good girls in the group who grew up parroting the expert and giving the right answer. It's been an invigorating experience for Sara, a beginning student.

> The best thing about improv is that you can't rehearse for it or study for it, so you don't put these expectations on yourself to be the best. You just go there and switch yourself on. I can't believe *I* did this routine where, one by one, we have to run into the middle of the room and sing. Any song. And give it the full treatment. I can't sing at all and the only thing I could think of was "Happy Birthday," but I belted it out. I put so much into that song my throat hurt. I know that moment was a breakthrough."

Many of the women in the group, including Diana and Sara, have adapted their improvisation skills to acting, lecturing, and writing. They dazzled themselves in the safe company of women, and then took their brave, new voices into their other worlds.

Up There On Your Own

Sara, who is a freelance writer, says that being on stage is not only better than therapy but it pushed her writing into a new direction. "For someone who hates confrontation and revealing what I really feel, this is so liberating because we confront in class all the time. And we get to express real emotions without someone saying we're being hysterical. Plus, I get to look inside me and create a fictional character and give her feelings and words."

A published short story came out of Sara's newfound freedom. "I created someone very different from me, like no one I know in my life. Being out there and not worrying about being judged opened me up. I wouldn't have dared create such an odd character in my stories before."

It's not just the stage performer who risks exposure. It's anyone who dares to stand alone. It costs something to put yourself out there where the public can have an opinion about you. The issues are similar for all women who break out of the modest, reserved, good-girl mold and emerge with a big voice.

The hundreds of thousands of women who took on the manufacturers of silicone implants had to quash a number of good-girl instincts in order to have their health concerns heard, all while discussing their breasts in court and on the nightly news.

Franny had to overcome a lifetime of conditioning that taught her not to question authority—"Starting with my doctor and all those other people who are supposed to know what's best for me." Franny said it was anger that gave her the courage to become a public spokeswoman on the controversial implants issue. "At first I was embarrassed to even have my name attached to the support group I formed. It was a big step from there to writing letters to the editor about how I felt about no longer having breasts but having my health."

In the end, Franny's and the others' voices were compelling enough to change medical procedure, alert the public to possible dangers, and put major manufacturers on notice that women were not going to be good little guinea pigs.

Stepping outside the private self really shakes up the good girl's tendency to blend into the wallpaper and not demand special attention. Stepping away from patterns can do the same. But, as Diana learned, while change is essential for growth, sometimes you have to start out small.

> I wanted to do something different. I wanted to do something with energy and heart. I talked to a friend and she said if I wanted to go in new directions that I first try changing the everyday stuff. Drive a different route to work. Get out of bed on the opposite side. Walk into my office and put my purse where I usually put my coffee cup. I started to see how enslaved we are to our habits. Changing them loosens our energy. That's one thing about improv, you come up against the rigid parts of yourself. There's a Buddhist teaching that says all things change when we do. After you leap and before you land, that's where God is.

Making changes and inviting the spotlight can bring in the critics, too. The ones outside as well as the ones from inside. "Sometimes I think oh shit, oh god, oh no, I have to do this," says Diana. "It's another version of the inner nag. 'You have nothing to offer.' 'Who do you think you are?' 'That is so dumb.' 'You're the worst one in here.' 'Everyone's going to call each other when they get home and rip on you.' But you know what? I realized *I* don't have to be great. It's not about being great. It's about doing something."

I started to see how enslaved we are to our habits. Changing them loosens our energy.

Perspective

In part because of her talent, in part because of who she is, and in part because people know what she's lived through, Diana has become a mentor to others, inspiring them to continue. When she says, "What do you have to lose?" the question carries weight.

When Sara protested that she didn't want to perform in the customary end-of-class performance for a small audience of friends and family, Diana looked at her sympathetically and then growled, "You don't have time for that shit." She later explained, "That has to stop mattering. We are so used to thinking that if we're not getting outside approval, we're not valuable. We're just annihilated by the worry that someone won't approve."

We are so used to thinking that if we're not getting outside approval, we're not valuable. We're just annihilated by the worry that someone won't approve.

Writer Anne Lamott expressed the same sentiment in a story where she is obsessing over whether her thighs are too big for a new skirt. Her friend, Pam, who's got terminal cancer, listens to her complain and then tells her that there's no time for "this shit," obsessing over the wrong thing. Sometimes worry is a big, unnecessary drain that's good for nothing.

But just walking to any stage brings back the familiar wobbly knees, dry mouth, and quaking stomach. Katharine Hepburn has admitted that she is almost physically sick before every performance. But Hepburn also has said that her jitters make her a better actress because she is never complacent and so is always trying her hardest.

Diana remembers being a wreck in college freshman speech class—"I could barely open my mouth"—and it's not much different now being on stage and waiting for the curtain to open. "Until the moment I actually step out on stage, I don't know if I can do it. It's terrifying . . . But it's so damned exciting. I try to think of it this way: I'm being asked to do something very scary. Oh, good."

I try to think of it this way: I'm being
asked to do something very scary. Oh, good.

Behind the Podium

It's a different kind of spotlight that shines on people in politics. When Jessica was elected to her city council she was stunned by what she called "the general lack of civility against people who basically volunteer their time to serve their community."

The always hot issue in Jessica's community is any project that pits environmental protection against economic growth. Because Jessica is a strong environmentalist and not shy about expressing her beliefs, she was routinely singled out by the opposition. She thinks, too, that her gender bothered her critics as much as her politics did. "I got in trouble for being assertive. Strong women make other people mad—and not just men." During Jessica's tenure, there were more editorials in the local paper about her than anyone else on the male-dominated council. She was chastised for misbehaving, being impolite, and Jessica says, "basically being a loudmouth." Of course, those in her corner thought she provided a needed spark to local politics.

The outspoken woman has an easier time today than she did in our foremothers' time, when opening your mouth could get you labeled a scold, a fishwife, or a shrew. But, still, any woman who dares to make noise is likely to risk offending someone. Or have someone say, "Who does she think she is?"

"We may have come a long way, but there's still a distinction between being strident and being stentorian, and it has to do with whether you're a woman or a man," says Jessica.

Stepping up to speak out feels hazardous for writers, too. Susan remembers when she first started writing an opinion column:

A friend in the business warned me that the toughest part was that I would become visible. I would expose myself, my ideas, even my family, and a lot more personal stuff than I did as a reporter. Stating your opinion invites people to disagree. And they do. They leave messages like, "Have you lost your mind?" It's taken me a while to accept that some people really don't like me. Good girls want most of all to be popular. But I tell myself that it would be pretty boring if we all agreed with each other. Different opinions serve to keep the dialogue going.

The good girl in you probably worries that there's always a critical audience out there, but it's possible that most people are really cheering you on. Pauline, Diana's improv teacher, believes that most audiences are welcoming. "I think what you have to remember when you're the person on stage," she says knowingly, "is how you feel when you're the person in the audience. You really are pulling for that singer or actor or comic. You don't want them to blow it. You want them to do well. To entertain you. You're even forgiving if there's a goof. That's a lot of love coming from out there. When you're on stage it's all coming to you. They are sitting there thinking, 'I wish I had the guts to do that.'"

While Sandy was camping with a group of women, some of whom knew her as a special education teacher, some who knew her as a cabaret singer, and some who hadn't met her before the trip, she was urged to sing one night after dinner. Without apology or embarrassed denial, she stepped forward and said she'd like to sing Joe Williams' "Here's to Life." As she stood there in sweatpants and flannel shirt, with no accompaniment but the crackle of the campfire, Sandy's voice filled the canyon like a dream. She owned that song. She owned the attention of all of those in her tiny audience. The response was beyond applause. The women all had tears in their eyes. They had not just listened to Sandy's song; they had listened to Sandy. Afterwards Sandy hugged everyone and said, "Thank you for crying."

8

SHELVING THE STORYBOOK ROMANCE

Letting Go of the Dream and Finding What's Real

And the crazy part of it was that even if you were clever, even if you spent your adolescence reading John Donne and Shaw, even if you studied history or zoology or physics and hoped to spend your life pursuing some difficult and challenging career—you still had a mind full of all the soupy longings that every high-school girl was awash in. It didn't matter, you see, whether you had an IQ of 170 or an IQ of 70, you were brainwashed all the same. Only the surface trappings were different. Only the talk was a little more sophisticated. Underneath it all, you longed to be annihilated by love. . . . Nobody bothered to tell you what marriage was really about. You weren't even provided, like European girls, with a philosophy of cynicism and practicality.

—Erica Jong, *Fear of Flying*

A Dream

It was a dream, a delicious feeling of abandon, filled with unconditional love. I got every girl's dream. A fairy princess wedding, a handsome, sweet man eager to please me. A honeymoon that filled my memory bank with exotic beauty. A first "home" complete with everything new. The dream got so comfortable I thought it would last forever . . . But the future has a way of falling in mid-flight.

Jazmin wrote those words in her divorce journal. Her dream-like marriage crumbled within a year of her storybook wedding, leaving her in a nightmare of shock and humiliation. After losing herself in the enchantment of love, however, she found a stronger version of herself that took her through her divorce. She chose not to run from the pain, but instead to ponder, talk with friends, and write about her experiences in her "divorce journal," which she shared with us for this book. Through the journal work, she discovered insights into herself and the nature of romantic love and she wanted to share what she had learned. If such a fall could happen to her, she feels, it could happen to anyone.

When she married, Jazmin was twenty-four years old, confident, bright, headed down a promising track, and appeared to the world to be a woman in charge of her own destiny. She is part of a generation of women well past the old-time notion that "you're nothing without a man." But conditioning runs deep. Even though she prided herself on her independence, Jazmin still had the good-girl quality of seeking approval from others. She found approval in the adoring eyes of Michael and then from others around them who celebrated the uniting of this handsome couple.

Jazmin describes their falling in love:

We met during an icebreaker at an orientation program to prepare students for the rigors of college. There was a game that had all participants shake hands, introduce themselves, and say a compliment to the next person. As everyone walked around the table in a raucous repeating of their names and saying compliments, I shook his hand and smiled my name, then told him he had the most beautiful eyes I'd ever seen. That was cupid's arrow I think. . . . He was sweet and playful and eager to please me in any way, from getting me ketchup at breakfast to carrying my books. On the last day of the program, as I sat on a couch falling asleep, he gently touched his lips to mine. . . .

We dated for the next couple of years, as we challenged our minds with new concepts and pulled all-nighters studying for exams or writing papers. He became my second half. Verbal communication was not always necessary, we had facial expressions to express ourselves secretly in crowded rooms. He made me feel completely, unconditionally loved. There was not an ounce of insecurity when I was with him, even if my hair was unwashed, or I had no makeup on and a big pimple had just erupted on top of my nose; he idolized me and constantly lavished me with tenderness.

Jazmin's love story characterizes the sweet dance of romantic courtship. We all know the dance. It begins with a certain look between two people from a distance (how many love songs feature that meeting of the eyes "across a crowded room"?), moves toward closeness as barriers fall away ("yeah, she's walkin' back to me"), and ends with the two becoming one ("ever since that night, we've been together.") Ah, falling in love. Intellectually, we know that's just a phase and the real relationship involves hard work, communication, and open eyes. But our heart may still respond to violins and roses more readily than the subtle frequencies of genuine connection. Since girlhood we've been listening to songs, reading books, and seeing movies that focus on courtship and end with the dream wedding.

The romantic imagery is so powerful that even women who ended bad marriages long ago can drift back into the memories of falling in love with their ex-husbands. Martha has been divorced for twenty-five years and, looking back, cannot imagine how she handled a twenty-year marriage to a man whose dogmatic opinions and criticisms stifled her so much when she was young. Still, she says, "When I hear certain songs or go to certain places we used to enjoy together, I can still feel a sentimental rush that leaves me momentarily limp, remembering that heady feeling of being ridiculously, blindly infatuated with that man."

Since girlhood we've been listening to songs, reading books, and seeing movies that focus on courtship and end with the dream wedding.

The Paperback Version

We don't have to look far to find sources for our cultural expectation that good girls fall in love, get that wedding, and wait for the rest to fall into place. Just look around the grocery store or airport and calculate the percentage of novels that revolve around the girl-meets-man-of-her-dreams plot. Many women are closet romance readers—stashing the Danielle Steel under the bed while they keep Joan Didion in the living room—secretly enjoying the satisfaction in an easily digested tale that will predictably serve a happily-ever-after dessert at the end. Even now, in the late nineties, one of the most popular books is about "the rules" of landing a man and the subterfuge it takes to hold on to him; that is, forget any idea of true connection and settle for manipulation to hook him into marriage. Popular culture emphasizes form over content. The paperback romance features sudden sparks, pounding hearts, turgid groins, and a few rounds of the back-and-forth, push-pull, turn-around, now-I've-got-you-now-I-don't dance that ends with the bride and groom going to the altar in a swirl of fairy dust. Tales of courtship still mesmerize, while less is told of what happens after the fairy dust has composted. How many of us remained dazzled by the images of Princess Di's royal wedding long after we came to know the sad reality behind it?

Wedding Pictures

For Jazmin, an elaborate wedding ceremony embraced both the American ideal of happily-ever-after and the traditions from her Mexican culture. As weddings do, Jazmin's extravaganza put the pressure on her to please everyone. She says, "It was like I was saying to others, 'I'm doing it my way but I'm doing what you asked.'"

Looking past the dreamy patina of one-time hopes, these days Jazmin can look at her wedding photo album and remember the part of her who was that bride. "Our wedding party consisted of fifty-two formally attired people, including the bride and groom, the maid of honor and best man, the padrinos of Velacion, arras, ramo, lazo, and anillos, and our parents. . . . It was a blending of Mexican and American traditions. It was a fairy tale. . . ."

A photographer documented the whole day in such artistic detail that, looking at the wedding album, Jazmin can almost experience the emotions again: the pride, the nervousness, the bubbling-over excitement of being The Bride with a four-foot train on her dress, her waist-length hair done up for the day and carefully arranged below a pearl-studded veil.

In one photograph, she is laughing, caught unawares in a moment of giddiness. In another, she is looking far away, with a pensive expression, as though something might be wrong. But she didn't know then what it was.

The Signals We Tune Out

In retrospect, Jazmin sees that there were warning signs that should have signaled trouble. Michael had difficulty holding down jobs. He was raised by a single mother and had no male role model to instill in him the value of sticking with family through difficult times. He was careless with money and acted like credit card debts would somehow take care of themselves. But with her own drive and sense of responsibility, Jazmin told herself she could be the breadwinner and Michael would be her supporter. In her idealized picture, they would balance one another out, without having to talk about it.

The pull of new love can be so strong, like a drug that blurs your vision and hides the obvious. The external "picture" seemed ideal, but privately, Jazmin had experienced her own doubts, even in the beginning. The look she had in that one wedding photograph helped her remember there were doubts even then. His adoration of her fueled the fairy-tale fantasy, but privately she wondered if she was losing herself in it. She remembers one time when she said to him, "I'm not sure that love lasts forever." Looking back, she wonders if her strong good-girl trait of preferring to be hurt rather than the other way around was responsible for stifling her doubts. Was she trying to push him away? Part of her was loving the romance. The other part was actually feeling ill.

> My biggest concern has always been hurting other people. That's what I meant when I asked about love lasting forever. In a way I was trying to warn him and warn myself. I did have doubts. I wondered, "What if my soul mate walks by and I'm already married?"
>
> I found myself carrying a lot in the relationship, without realizing it or acknowledging myself for it. Internally, I wanted out, I wanted the freedom to be responsible for only myself, but I was conditioned to be a "good woman." It was too selfish to think of myself, and I knew I would never want the responsibility of leaving, failing at my role as wife. So I got sick instead, with headaches and menstrual cramps, lethargy and lack of interest. I was slowly losing my zest and awe of life, becoming a stagnant, heavy person. This ended up pushing him away and led him to choose a new path. I suffered and wept, but at some level thanked him for his courage. I wouldn't have been able to leave him, and it felt better to be the "victim." I think he knew that I wouldn't leave, too faithful to my cultural upbringing, too afraid to purposely hurt someone else to make myself happy.

Jazmin had physical symptoms of her unhappiness in the marriage, but at the time didn't recognize them for what they were. The weight of needing to be the "ideal couple" was too strong. She didn't want to be responsible for shattering that. Good girls often get sick before they break up relationships.

Another woman, Virginia, paid attention to her physical symptoms—before the wedding bells. She recalls her engagement to a man who seemed like an ideal mate: good-looking, successful, and enamored with her. But she found herself getting frequent stomachaches, a vague gnawing at her insides, when she was with him. She was raised in a stoic German family. "No one talked much about emotions. But I knew something was wrong." Against her family's wishes, she broke the engagement. She couldn't explain the reasons to him, to her family, or even to herself. She just knew she couldn't stand that tight feeling in her stomach anymore. She thought maybe she would never marry. Then she met a man who made her laugh and feel content. With him, she felt herself. It wasn't until then that she saw how much was missing in her first engagement.

Of course, true love stories begin after the glitter goes away and reality settles in. Suddenly, you're dealing with moods, limits, quirks, bills, and bathroom habits. The real-life plot involves finding some way to cope with all your differences and life's curves and still hang on to a trace of that spark. But that means letting go of the ideal, facing problems head-on, risking disapproval, and maybe having an occasional noisy fight. Not good-girl behavior at all. Marie, who has a solid marriage of fifteen years, says it's not about perfection but commitment to handle anything that comes up. "Sometimes we want to strangle each other, other times we have those romantic feelings like when we were dating. Sex is part of it, but it's not everything. We have friendship and trust and love that I think can stand up to anything. Humor helps, too. We tell each other a lot of gross jokes."

Jazmin never got past the courtship phase, where you make believe everything is beautiful. Looking back, she sees how her desire to maintain the image of the perfect couple kept her and Michael from handling anything negative that came up.

In Jazmin's reflections, Michael does not emerge as the sole problem. For her, it was as much the social expectations of what it means to be married in a society where girls are raised on "happily ever after" but don't necessarily receive training in how to maintain their own identities in the process.

These days she's not looking for Prince Charming. She enjoys stories about successful relationships that have rocky beginnings rather than the blind plunge into deceptively smooth waters.

The real-life plot involves finding some way to cope with all your differences and life's curves and still hang on to a trace of that spark.

What, Me Marry?

With the cultural pressure toward marriage, it's refreshing to find women who rebel against the idea. When this kind of independent woman does enter a relationship, it's because she has found something solid and real. And she is convined she won't lose herself.

When Judith was a little girl, she watched her father and a neighbor cut down her mother's favorite tea plant. "She was crying. And I decided I never wanted to be in that position." Judith wasn't about to take any risks with a man and she resolved never to marry. At twenty-two, she had a dream that a man was carrying her off against her will. In the dream, she remembers patting her Volkswagen goodbye and whispering, "I cannot take you now. I'll come back." For Judith, marriage meant giving something up. It wasn't just her mother's tea plant. Her mother had always wanted to be a journalist, but never pursued her career. "She didn't even have a notebook. She had babies instead." Judith managed to escape the temptations of matrimony over the years, but in her thirties she fell for a man hard enough to slowly weave her life together with his. Over a period of months, they moved toward a shared household. They even began working together, sharing space for her window-covering business and his upholstery business. "But we are not legal business partners. That would require a contract." Contracts or no, they've shared their days and their nights for years now. Judith helped him raise his children, although she doesn't have any interest in having children of her own. "I'm still waiting to hear from my biological clock. I don't think it has batteries."

Some women have found ways to mine bad experiences for wisdom about what lies between perfection and hopelessness. Women who go on to find new, more earthly romances after the fall from ideal love tend to be those who aren't so quick to dump the good memories from the bad relationships.

"I'm still waiting to hear
from my biological clock.
I don't think it has batteries."

When she found out her husband was having an affair with her best friend, Jane felt her heart break and her stomach churn so violently she couldn't keep food down. Her daughter was only in the fourth grade, so she decided to stick the marriage out. But she grew stronger, less dependent, and eventually had an affair of her own. She ended up leaving her husband and marrying her lover. Her second marriage is more reality-based but it's also a much better romance, she says. Would she have found this man if she had allowed herself to be embittered toward all men because of her first husband's flaws? "After divorce, you don't need to negate the memories to let go of the marriage. And you can look back and count up all the good things that your ex made possible. I tell my daughter that had it not been for her father, I would never have developed into the person I am today . . . and I would never have had her. Maybe we fall daffy in love with the wrong person just long enough to produce the wonderful child."

After divorce, you don't need to negate
the memories to let go of the marriage.

Fight for the Real

Often women find a companionable partner after years of dating, when they start considering people who don't match their old idea of Mr. Right. Audrey says when she first met her ideal mate, he was anything but a candidate for matrimony. "We immediately clicked with each other, but had different ideas about the future." Before she met him, she had given up on the idea that she had to be married to have children, and was raising a son on her own. She wanted more children. He was ambivalent. She liked year-round warm and sunny climates; he liked moderate temperatures and frequent rain. Audrey says she felt comfortable enough with herself that she could focus on enjoying their time together rather than fixating on the happily-ever-after. "I trusted my instincts that our love was real even if he had trouble with commitment. It took years for him to feel ready for marriage—and we made a few other compromises." They ended up settling in a place with dry summers and rainy winters. "Both of us were past thirty when we got together," Audrey says. "I think age was a factor in our favor. We were young enough to still feel the power of lust, but old enough to know that lust isn't enough. We both were too set in our ways to simply 'give in,' but we were enough in love that we couldn't walk away. So we worked things out—before we got married. It took years."

When she hears Audrey's story, Jazmin smiles. She likes the image of a woman solid in herself—not in a rush. She looks back at how she once felt the need to be merged into a couple, so completely that she could not entertain any of the nagging worries that something was wrong. She came to depend on the illusion that everything was "perfect" until one day she was feeling ill at a party, and Michael suggested she go home—without him. She was shocked at his sudden indifference. Her stomach pains were so bad, she ended up going to the hospital. Her father drove her because Michael was still out partying. It turned out to be nothing serious, but the episode infuriated her. Angrily, she said, "Maybe we just shouldn't be together." Calmly, he said, "You're right." He left. She was shocked, anguished, but too proud to call him back. She started writing letters to him in a journal, confident he would return and she could show him. It wasn't until weeks later that he came to see her. He told her he thought he was holding her back in life. It was from a mutual friend that she later learned that he was having an affair. The notebook in which she had been writing to Michael turned into her divorce journal. One poem, in English and Spanish, captured the unreal sensations she had when she saw him a month after their goodbye.

You look like the same person.
Pero no eras. [But you are not the same.]
I want to talk to you.
Y ya no existes. [And you do not exist.]
I want to talk and share.
Y tu ya no apareces. [And you do not appear to me.]
I can't cry because you're still alive.
Y no entiendo que ya no vives. [And you are not alive to me.]
I want you back to wake with me.
Pero tu ya estas en otro mundo. [But you are in another world.]
You look like the same person.
Pero eres otro. [But you are someone else.]

Returning to the Self

Jazmin's poem captures the end of her fantasy. These days she is trying to avoid projecting romantic fantasies onto men. She distrusts almost any tingly sensation that reminds her of how she felt before she was swept away. She figures it will be awhile before she can trust herself.

Many women have found that the first step is to recognize where they picked up their notion of the idealized romance. It took years for Holly, a police officer, to recognize how she'd been programmed for relationship disaster. But it didn't take long after her realization for something real to fill the void left when she gave up her more impossible fantasies.

> I think I got my ideas about love from reading Camelot stories and Gothic romances. It was all about suffering, about longing for the lover who was unattainable, unavailable. It was exciting, sad ... tragic. And that describes most of my relationships. They were torrid. I got involved in impossible triangles. I'd swing from highs to lows. I held on to one doomed relationship for years, then somehow I finally broke free. Then I did something levelheaded and so normal it was weird. I let a friend set me up with a man she said was "really nice." Nice. That was no recommendation in my book. Well, not in my old book. I was ready for something new. Why not someone nice? We hit it off immediately. It wasn't that shock kind of attraction, but something warmer and more

comfortable. I thought, "This feels right." It was like coming home.

They were married within a year and now have three children.

The old style ideal marriage, be it according to Jane Austen or a paperback romance, usually demands a man who makes more money, is taller, older, and a challenge to get. For Holly, the real man behind the fantasy turned out to be a little younger, making less money, and was as happy to be found as she was to find him.

Recognizing "Mr. Right" when he isn't like anyone we recognize from books or media usually happens after women have let go of the old culturally imposed images. And after they have let go of some of their good-girl expectations.

Jazmin knows she has a long way to go before she'll be able to see her way clearly in the dating circuit. For now, she is turning for inspiration to a different part of her cultural tradition—art. In her drawings, she is depicting healers and wise women from Mexican mythology. At the same time, she is pampering herself with a lot of rest, exercise, and time out with girlfriends. Her migraine headaches and fierce menstrual cramps ceased when Michael left her, leaving her feeling better physically than she had felt since her marriage.

> We were young enough to still feel the power of lust, but old enough to know that lust isn't enough. We both were too set in our ways to simply "give in," but we were enough in love that we couldn't walk away.

Only One at Your Table, Miss?

For the time being, Jazmin is cozying into single status, learning to enjoy her own company, and consciously rejecting the stigma that our couple-oriented culture places on the woman alone. Recently she walked into a restaurant and the maître d' looked past her for another. No one was with her. "Just one?" he asked. "Of course!" she replied. It's a familiar experience. Maybe you're married but on a solo adventure. Maybe you're between relationships. Maybe you've chosen the single life. But whatever the reason you're alone, out in public you sense some social disapproval. Aren't good girls supposed to be on the arm of a man, preferably with children in tow? Lynn, who loves her independence, grows weary of the social emphasis on mates and offspring. "When I'm at a social gathering, it's amazing to me how much of people's conversation revolves around spouses and children. It's not that I'm disinterested, but as a single woman, I feel like an outsider."

Although Toni is married, her husband travels a lot, leaving her to experience the single life. While she feels at ease socializing alone, she admits to some pride in being part of a "couple." "I found myself asking him to rearrange his schedule to attend events that didn't interest him very much. He challenged my motives, and I admitted there was more than my pleasure in his company. Of course it's more fun to be together, but sometimes it was also about appearances. That admission bothered me, so I started looking for pleasure in going places solo. Where I work, a lot of people joke that I only have a phantom husband."

The couple-orientation of our culture leads women to feel that having a mate is a source of security, an accomplishment. It can even become a competition among women who have consciously or unconsciously accepted the cultural value that marriage is a sign of success.

The popular media has certainly perpetuated some myths that would seem to be upping the ante for the competition. For example, the notions that all good men are taken and, especially beyond a certain age, women might as well give up trying to find a partner worth their while. That makes dating seem like a game of musical chairs where the "winners" have gotten theirs by the time the music has stopped.

The pressure to pair up is palpable for many women, but there are those who recognize the need to break free, at least for a while. They take the time to sort out fantasy from reality and to recognize whether the voice whispering in their ears is urging them to follow their hearts or diverting their attention from their true selves, urging them to slip into the familiar roles women know so well.

In one of the last entries in her divorce journal, Jazmin wrote, "In spite of being such a lonely number, One is strong and erect and tall. One is solid and long and secure; no leaning to ask for support. It feels lonely being single again. But more sturdy than a wobbly two."

The pressure to pair up is palpable for many women, but there are those who recognize the need to break free, at least for a while.

9

No More Ms. Perfect

Letting Go of Having It All Together and Enjoying Your Imperfections

When she stopped conforming to the conventional picture of femininity she finally began to enjoy being a woman.

—Betty Friedan

Even those whose lives had appeared to be ticking imperturbably under their smiling clock-faces were often trying, like me, to evolve another rhythm with more creative pauses in it, more adjustment to their individual needs and new and more alive relationships to themselves as well as others.

—Anne Morrow Lindbergh

There are many realities. We should remember this when we get too caught in being concerned about the way the rest of the world lives or how we think they live.

—Natalie Goldberg

Don't Look Too Close

Carla is a mother, wife, and high-powered professional in the field of healthcare. On the home front, she's a woman who prides herself on knowing how to make a bed with hospital corners so perfect they would put a drill sergeant to shame. The idea of the floor being so clean you could eat off it is not a cliché for Carla—it is a standard. A standard she knows how to meet, and, indeed, did meet for years. She would probably still be living up to it now, if only she had the time. The floor needs to be mopped. But it's late, she's been working all day, and she's tired. And, of course, she'd have to do it right, which means getting out the special little throw rug she keeps for protecting her knees as she kneels down to scrub the floor by hand. Doing it right means having a knife at her side for those stubborn sticky spots, and a can of cleanser for those pesky stains. Cleaning the floor is no small chore, it's a war against dirt, and you must be armed. She can almost feel the internal drumroll that mobilizes her for a frontal assault against the dirt. But then a relatively new voice speaks from her mind, "Give it up, girl!" So instead of waging war on her knees, she gets out a squeeze-mop and fills a pail. She doesn't worry about the ground-in stains or the dust she knows is lurking in the corner. She makes a quick pass over the floor, escapes the scene of the crime, puts it out of her mind, and happily goes upstairs to bed to join her husband. It's something she'd never have done a few years ago. There's a twinge of guilt, a remnant of days gone by. But, she tells herself—almost, but not quite, believing it—no one's perfect.

> No matter how equally we divide the domestic labors, it usually seems as though the domain of hearth and home is ultimately the woman's responsibility.

Next to Godliness

Carla's a fanatical example of a woman with a domestic work ethic that once bordered on tyranny. She got over it, and tells how later in this chapter. For Carla, and many others, order at home has been a metaphor for the orderly life. And that's a big issue.

When women start talking with one another about attitudes toward housework and order, it's like peeking under each other's rugs and getting a glimpse at the real dirt—the dusty dregs of guilt left over from the messages we've heard from generations past about what it means to have a tidy life. Cautionary phrases that are familiar to most of us are variations on themes that ruled many of our mothers and grandmothers.

> If you wear torn underwear and get in an accident, everyone in the hospital will see that you're a slob.

> If all the girls in the locker room see a pin in your bra strap, they'll think you're poor.

> If you let your kids make tents in the living room out of blankets, one of the neighbors—or perhaps the Queen of England—may drop by and see that your household is truly out of control.

> There are microscopic bugs that start hatching within a minute of exactly one week after you last changed the sheets on your bed.

> No one would ever eat your cookies if they could see the baking pan you used.

> You never know when a party guest will pull open the shower curtain to make sure you've cleaned the bathtub.

No matter how equally we divide the domestic labors, it usually seems as though the domain of hearth and home is ultimately the woman's responsibility. If someone's critical of your house, it's your fault.

The concepts of Cleanliness-is-next-to-Godliness and a-place-for-everything-and-everything-in-its-place are standards left over from a sterner era. But these days they're impossible priorities for women who are balancing motherhood, marriage, career, social life, community work, and running a household—or even just two out of six.

The overachiever gets tangled up in her need to be the perfect everything. Thoughtful mother forgets the flowers she promised to deliver to her son's drama teacher the first night of the school play because she was on deadline for her almost-perfect novel whose pages she had scattered through her usually-tidy living room just as her husband brought home surprise dinner guests to be fed and entertained by his always gracious wife.

The archetypal Ms. Perfect prides herself on gleaming floors and an equally shiny career. Ms. Perfect is the Good Girl Run Amok, the woman who seeks to conform to the ideal in all aspects of her life, scrambling to appear all together —doing her best and more. She is the woman who wants to get a score of ten on the scale of life. She can't do anything half way. She can't rest. She's not sure why. She knows some of it is external. And some of it is herself saying, "If you're perfect, no one can criticize you."

Ms. Perfect tries so hard that she loses perspective. As she scratches activities off her things-to-do list, she doesn't stop to figure out what's really important. Lunch with a friend is right there next to feeding the geraniums which is next to a romantic dinner which is next to taking the dog for his shots.

One day Toni, a writer, started listing how many different roles she played in life and how she might improve each one.

> I wanted to be Mary Poppins with the kids. You know, that sunny presence singing "Just a spoonful of sugar . . ." and helping life be smooth for everyone. In dealing with agents and editors I wanted to be one of those coolly competent, no-nonsense Nora Ephron types. But then to write creatively I imagined myself a spontaneous, eccentric artist, a combination of Janis Joplin, Georgia O'Keefe, and Virginia Woolf, doing my work without giving a damn what the world thinks. At the same time I was trying to be Mother Teresa to my friends, Julia Child in the kitchen, and Pretty Woman in the bedroom.
>
> I keep that list at the back of my appointment book to look at on days when I wonder why I'm feeling overwhelmed and inadequate. It makes me laugh.

There are women who have picked through the detritus of long-lost impossible expectations of themselves and emerged feeling clean in spirit, even with sticky stuff left on their baseboards. They've found ways to let go of the vague notion that there is some external standard of order, and they've grabbed on to what's really important to them—the brass ring of good relationships and meaningful work. For some, including Carla, it took a mini-breakdown to get her priorities straight.

Idle Fingers

There was a time when Carla would no more have done an overeasy mop job than she would have walked down the street naked. For her, a perfectly scrubbed house was a symbol of internal discipline and impeccable credentials as a good person, mother, and wife. If someone called her compulsive, she would smile with her lovely white teeth, her brown eyes would flash, and with a tinkling laugh she would say, "Thank you." She was raised in a family of four girls by a single mother who drilled into them the adage "Idle fingers make for trouble."

Carla was Ms. Clean and General Control rolled into one, with two healthy sons, an R.N. degree, and a promising future in healthcare management. Her second husband had four children of his own, and suddenly she found herself in a chaotic household with six children and complexities she never imagined.

> I was trying not only to have a career that was upwardly mobile, but making sure the kids were getting good grades and, of course, reflecting well on me. I had so many goals that were conflicting and I could not meet all of them. I also wanted to be able to have fun, for all of us to love each other, and be in an atmosphere of good humor. I wanted to be an affirming mother. Instead I was hollering and screaming about how the house looked.

Carla'a demanding routine was exhausting. She vacuumed the bathroom walls once a week. Every night dinner was a three-course meal. But she wasn't getting much cooperation in her new household of six kids under the age of fourteen. And it made her furious. "I felt completely out of control."

Carla had grown up with a regimen established by her mother, who worked, but set up a system whereby every square inch of the house would regularly get a thorough cleaning. It almost made sense in the rural area where she was raised. If the cupboards weren't cleaned, spiders and bugs would get into the flour. But along with the practical reasons for cleanliness, there was her mother's expectation that the house would be taken care of in her absence during the day. Carla absorbed the "Cleanliness next to Godliness" ethic unquestioningly. As a child, she found that it was easier to keep her room clean if she worked at it daily. "I didn't like not being able to find my stuff. It became clear to me that it was easier to keep order by working regularly. And I found the discipline liberating."

The discipline served her well during her first marriage. She married a seminary student and had to adapt to small quarters. She told people she could make a neat, clean, and attractive home anywhere. "Having things pretty was important to me." For a time, she and her husband lived in her sister-in-law's converted garage. "I created a little home out there, a little nest."

But as the years passed, Carla and her husband moved out into the world of work and their own home. Responsibilities multiplied, houses were bigger, children came, and it grew more difficult to keep everything "just so." Carla's perfectionism was one point of conflict in the marriage, but eventually it was dwarfed by more significant differences.

The only consolation she took from her devastating divorce was that she had one less pair of socks to pick up off the floor and freedom to create a household that reflected her own sense of order. That changed when she fell in love with Daniel, who would become her second husband. Carla told herself she had the organizational ability to manage a household of six children. What she didn't count on was the emotional effort it would take to convince members of her new family to conform to her standards. When it became clear that she simply could not impose her immaculate ways on others, she started to come apart.

> My breakdown came one day when I was getting ready to leave work for home. I was so depressed. I didn't want to go home because I didn't know what I would find. I'd rather move out of the house than find dishes in the sink. I could not deal with this household. That night, my husband and I had a long talk, and I came to some hard realizations about my obsession with perfection. It was my fear that chaos would break out. If my children

were living in a hovel and not eating good meals, people would think I was a bad mother.

Daniel and I talked about making some compromises and the next day we had a family conference. I was ready to agree to some trade-offs. I would allow TV dinners in the freezer. That way, the kids could get nourishment at any time without leaving dirty dishes. I agreed to let the kids keep their rooms any way they wanted—I wouldn't even open their doors—as long as they would divide up chores to keep the shared downstairs area neat. We agreed to get everything done during the week so we could have weekends together. Having fun together became a priority. I've lowered my standards a lot.

**Having fun together became a priority.
I've lowered my standards a lot.**

Straight A's

Good-girl perfectionism starts young. Smart good girls figure out how to please the teacher. Throughout life there's some benefit that comes from understanding the system and knowing how to work it. But real learning comes from knowing the teacher's standard isn't always the only one.

Rose is a college student who's accustomed to getting A's, but as she was graduating she started to separate what she needed to do to please her professors from what she needed to do to satisfy herself.

In getting good grades, you're trying to do a paper or project a certain way. There's a formula. You know there is a professor who will be judging it. The grade is the reward. But then I did a video project where I realized I was doing it to please me. My ultimate goal was to be happy with it instead of making it to impress someone else. There isn't a formula for that. I told myself that this has got to feel good for me. I spent a lot of time with that video. I got into it. I was open, the work was more free-flowing and exciting. When you're trying to meet someone else's standards, it's stressful the whole time. When you're doing it for yourself, it's still stressful, but there are moments of real fun and excitement. It's intoxicating.

The perfectionist is so accustomed to following everyone else's rules she doesn't allow for much self-expression. Lucky for Rose she's figuring this out at a pretty young age. "I think it's fine to be a perfectionist on some things, but I want to choose which ones."

Ms. Perfect works inside the box, the place where there are defined parameters and rules that tell us how far we can go. We reach a certain age and start to wonder who made the rules and why we're still trying so hard to follow them.

"There were so many rules when I was growing up," says Jeannie. "No singing at the table. What was that about?"

Many women now find some satisfaction in an articulate statement of their bottom line.

Flakes

On the opposite end of the perfect scale are those who just can't seem to "get it together." Chaos reigns, in the form of mountains of laundry, piles of unopened mail, and a clock that seems to perpetually scream out, "You're late again!" Making a foray into the garage to go through boxes is like an archeology expedition. Sometimes it's easier to just forget it: sit down and read a book, go out for the day, or find an uncluttered patch on the floor and play a game of checkers with your kid.

Humor helps, as well as talking to friends who admit to their own daily messes. There's sanity to be found in trading war stories about the disaster-scale episodes involved simply in getting out the door, or having a friend look in your vegetable bin and comment, "My, how clever of you to keep your compost in the refrigerator!"

Women are often plagued by memories of their own mothers' perfection, nonworking mothers with June Cleaver's expertise in the domestic arts. Letting go means realizing that we have different values than previous generations, when some women measured their worth by the sparkle of their stemware.

"I'm not my mother," says Rhonda, a working mom, coming to terms with the fact that she'll never have every room in her house perfectly neat and clean at the same time. "A lot of my childhood memories are of my mother vacuuming. She spent her time keeping the house really clean. Too clean."

Many women now find some satisfaction in an articulate statement of their bottom line. Rhonda has carpets of a well-chosen brown, exactly the color of the dirt around her country home. She has nooks and crannies where messes can be intentionally hidden if certain relatives drop by. "I keep my house tidy," she says, then adds with a laugh, "well, there's nothing gross that would alert the public health department."

Saturday morning is cleanup day, and cleanliness is a relative matter. "If you saw my kids' rooms you might not call them clean, but they're at a different stage from where they started. My son's idea of cleaning is putting everything on a table. Everybody has their own level of acceptable. Mine is that I can't handle dirty bathrooms and the kitchen table has to be clear."

The trade-off is clear. To make her life perfect, she'd have to go around working on tasks that take time away from the good stuff. "I like to goof around with my friends; we do lots of family things on the weekends. I don't have any regrets about how I choose to spend my time. If anything I wish I could let go of a little more. I still do get uptight," says Rhonda.

One thing that does bother her is keeping track of all her belongings. Her home has become the museum for family heirlooms, storage for her extended family. "I'm incapable of throwing anything out," she says. Thus, there are boxes and stacks and closets full of items to be sorted, as well as items she put away that she'd love to use, if only she could remember where she put them. "There are some things I'll never find, some things I may find, if I have an idea where to look. These days not only can I not find my own things but I can't find my children's things. I found an old Christmas present that I had hidden so well it didn't turn up until the next November."

Justine, a single mother, isn't exactly a neat-freak and regularly finds mysterious piles to be sorted, but she feels that she has a comfortable level of order. "I've gotten over that a clean house should be anything beyond what I have the energy to do. I suspect, though, I wouldn't feel that way if I had a man in my house; then I think I'd feel more pressure."

Joy, who lives on a ranch, says, "I have to get along with my husband, so I keep my house other than I would on my own. If I lived alone, I'd have piles of books everywhere. I'm neat, but I'm nowhere near perfect. I figure, 'Love me; love my mess.' If it's really important to someone how I keep my house, we're probably not going to make a connection anyway."

One thing friends do for each other is model tolerance. Justine has some friends who live with almost total disorder, but when she's at their house she goes with the flow, clearing off a space to sit and accepting the mess. "I don't want my house to look like that, but it's okay with me if they do."

I figure, "Love me; love my mess."
If it's really important to someone how
I keep my house, we're probably not
going to make a connection anyway.

But What If the Queen Drops By?

The problem comes when there's a gap between a woman's expectations of herself and what she can actually do. It's freeing to accept that you can only do "so much," but sometimes circumstances demand more.

There's that old fear that someone of great import might "drop by" and see the stacks of newspapers piling up on the table or the hamper overflowing. For Natalie, the feared guest is anyone with "more money than I have who I assume has the luxury of a perfect house." For Shea, it's any man or woman from the older generation whom she assumes has a higher standard for neatness.

Barbara lived with the reality that a persnickety, critical guest might drop by at any moment when she put her house on the market—and it took two years to sell. She had to be ready, all the time, for a potential buyer to drop by and scrutinize any corner of the house, from insides of closets to the baseboards. "I'd been messy since birth, but suddenly we could not be messy. We were always ready for the realtors. I never saw the house through my own eyes. You look at everything differently. I was always fluffing up the pillows on the couch."

After they moved to a house in the country, Barbara could define her own standards. "That home was a forty-five-minute drive from town, and visitors would get to a crossroads where I told them to call to get directions to the house. That gave me exactly fifteen minutes to make the house presentable."

These days, Barbara lives in town again but she still can straighten the house into acceptability in fifteen minutes.

Sorry, No More Apologies

Ironically, Ms. Perfect can never claim perfection. That would be immodest. She's knocking herself out to excel at everything, but at the same time must show humility. "That was a great report, you must have worked all weekend," a co-worker says. Ms. Perfect must dismiss it with some variation of "aw shucks, it's nothing." Or if it's truly award-winning, she can defuse the compliment by undermining herself— "My poor family ate TV dinners all weekend, and you should see the laundry pile!"

Humility, we learned young, is up there at the top of good-girl virtues. Acting conceited is a serious flaw. But if you minimize your hard work, you'll eventually convince others that what you've done really isn't such a big deal. There are some cures for the humility syndrome. The first step is a simple "thank you," which is a difficult response for good girls. It takes practice to accept compliments. For advanced students, there's self-praise.

Martha learned it in midlife. "I really shocked my grandson when I told him how proud I was of a painting I finished. He said, 'Grandma, you're bragging.' I said, 'Yep, I sure am.' He seemed to think that was a delightful idea."

Humility has been practiced by women for generations, considered part of a gentle and meek nature. So, naturally, by the time it got to the current generation, we were accustomed to saying "I'm sorry" indiscriminately and without thinking. One morning Toni decided to count the number of times she apologized in the day. She quit after six—and it was only midmorning. "There's always something to be sorry about. Where does that come from? I keep thinking of an that Golda Meir quote, 'Don't be so humble; you're not that great.' Where did I get the idea that people will like me more if I'm self-effacing?"

Jodie, a travel agent, figured out what fueled her humility and decided to let it go. "It took me a few years but I finally gave myself permission to shine. I always worried that if something good happened to me it would make others feel bad. Now, my business is doing well, and I'm successful and I say it's okay to have abundance. I always keep in mind a line from the character Sug in Alice Walker's novel *The Color Purple*: 'Flowers don't apologize for being purple.'"

Repeat After Me: "Perfunctory"

In high school, "perfunctory" sounded like a bad word and something a high achiever would never want to be—routine, ordinary, not very creative. But it comes in handy for the Ms. Perfect who obsesses over every detail and becomes a slave to ridiculously high expectations. We can always do a little more work, add another small task, push ourselves a little bit harder. But sometimes we're pouring our energy into someone else's cup.

It's okay to not make it perfect every time, to forget that last phone call so you can leave work just a little early. To serve your dinner guests take-out food. To light candles, build a fire, and leave the lights low so you don't have to vacuum.

Listen to Ms. Perfect's lackadaisical sister, Ms. Perfunctory. She'll tell you that "okay" is sometimes good enough. Loosen those standards from time to time and breathe.

Heloise Revisited

Our mothers may have traded "Hints from Heloise" about how to keep a house, but these days many of us are trading our sleight-of-hand, now-you-see-it-now-you-don't tricks for keeping the surface of our lives looking clean.

"My kitchen counter is loaded with things I'm going to deal with 'any time now,' but instead it's growing at fantastic proportions," says Joy. "A friend of mine taught me a trick, just put a dish towel over the mess if someone comes over."

Lynn believes in designated piles. It may look chaotic to someone walking in, but she knows exactly where to find that blueprint. The question is—how long will it take? "I have to know where things are to the extent that I can retrieve them in a reasonable period of time. The time limit is the variable. For some things, I can live with a twenty-minute retrieval time. If I may need it in ten minutes, it goes somewhere else. The outer layer is stuff I need right away."

Toni has a solution to both filing and neatening her desk at home. Every so often she takes a cardboard box to do a "quick sort." She pulls out the items that must be handled—such as correspondence that, if unanswered, would result in debtor's prison, ruining a relationship, or missing out on a contract for her business. Then she puts the rest into a box and dates it. That way, if she thinks of something she needs from that time period, she knows where to look. Most of the time, she doesn't need to go back.

Domestic Specialists

Although few women these days have the ability, time, or desire to be perfect domestic engineers, many of us enjoy aspects of housekeeping that bring pride, pleasure, a sense of relaxation, and sometimes a diversion from other aspects of life that are less easy to control.

For Natalie, the occasional whirlwind cleaning jag is a welcome reprieve from difficult family circumstances. "Sometimes cleaning messes helps me deal with things I can't deal with at all. I have a mother who is dying, a father who is ill. So what do

I do when my husband and I are on vacation at the beach? I clean up the whole cottage. It really helped. There was nothing I could do for my parents, but I could clean those floors. When I can't accomplish the big things, I do the little things."

Most women have household activities they find soothing. Toni makes most of her friends gag when she goes on about how much she loves to iron. "There's something delightful about getting those wrinkles out, making a collar perfect by starting at the very edge, just like my mother taught me, and working inward. I like it when you fill the iron with water and that blast of steam comes out. It's like, 'We're going to get down to business here.' When I wear freshly pressed clothes, I feel like I'm really together."

"I love to sweep," says Barbara. "I have hardwood floors and I love the broom in my house. I'm not big on dusting, but I love to sweep."

June loves the smell of freshly laundered clothes and finds folding and putting the laundry away a source of pleasure. Just don't ask her to mend anything.

The New Network

When women become more honest with one another, often they find ways to help each other out with private messes. This is a friendly collaboration, where you can admit your failings, strut your skills, and have some fun while getting chores done.

For Toni, the network was activated when she found herself sorting through boxes of things that had belonged to her grandparents and other family members who were no longer alive. Each object seemed to carry a memory or feeling that had to be sorted out along with the objects. One day her friend Marie offered to help. "Just tell me what to throw away," Toni said. Having someone at her side helped her to let go of the things while keeping the memories.

Marie enjoys whipping around the house and getting things organized, Toni doesn't know where to begin. Marie has the job of ironing her husband's shirts, Toni's husband insists on handling his own permanent press laundry, even though she'd love to take an iron to them. One day they hit on the idea of an exchange. Marie brought her ironing over, and Toni happily set about steaming them to perfection while Marie organized the chaos of pots, pans, and dishes in Toni's kitchen. They laughed, told jokes, and listened to music full blast.

"It's our dirty little secret," Toni says. "Our husbands would probably be mortified to find out that we have seen inside each other's cupboards, and most of our friends would think we're nuts. But we keep doing it and getting better at it. Lately, we've been cooking double amounts and trading dinners—taking full credit for each other's culinary successes."

10

WE ARE NOT OUR STUFF

Letting Go of Keeping It All and Holding On to What's Worthwhile

I want real things—music that makes holes in the sky.

—Georgia O'Keefe

To move freely you must be deeply rooted.

—Bella Lewitzsky

Carolyn gazed out over the Pacific and looked toward a different life. She didn't know what she was getting into, but she knew what she'd given up—a prestigious job, a big house, and all the things she'd once coveted. She'd learned the importance of ritual from some of her former therapy clients, who marked major life changes with quiet ceremony. She was by herself, sitting on a plot of land that would contain her new scaled-down life. She'd taken shelter from the rain in the small cabin on the property. She was alone. Her husband had gone back to the city, leaving her to mull over this dramatic move in their lives. "Suddenly," she said, "the moon broke through the clouds. I was able to walk outside and light three candles. To look ahead. And to let go of what I'd been. What I had. What I thought I had to be."

The Nudge You Need

The ideal of having it all has become a cultural norm. "She who has the most clothes when she dies, wins," says the bumper sticker. So the woman who one day looks up and decides she doesn't want or need some of her possessions, be they a big house or, in Carolyn's case, a big job, has some explaining to do—to herself and the rest of the world, which awards status points for having "more."

This challenges the good-girl instinct to do well according to someone else's value system. It means rejecting the trappings that society says are important, which thereby forces the individual to decide for herself what's most precious. Just as the media tells us how to look it also shows us how success is supposed to look, and anything less than grand it's not.

Two years before her candle ritual, Carolyn was driving down a road in Denver, going about ten miles per hour on black ice, when a truck hit a car that rammed her car off the road onto the sidewalk. "I realized I could have died. I had soft tissue injury, back, neck, and head injury. I needed therapy every single day. I was pretty miserable." Her recovery took nine months; so she had a lot of time to reflect on whether she wanted to keep living her life the same way.

At the time of her accident Carolyn was a psychotherapist specializing in working with sexual abuse survivors—satisfying, well-paid work that earned her a respected place in the community. She was often called on to give expert testimony in court. But the work was exhausting. "The last six years I'd concentrated mostly on child victims. It was painful, difficult work."

She and a partner had run their own agency for ten years. Carolyn billed two hundred dollars an hour for testifying in court. She made a good amount of money a year. Her husband had an equally well-paying job as an airline pilot. They lived in the suburbs in a sprawling house, took long vacations to Bali and Australia, and ate most dinners out. "That was probably one of the biggest changes in coming here—learning how to cook all over again."

The couple now live in a small town on the coast, a onetime fishing port. Carolyn's husband still flies for an airline, and she runs their downscaled life while picking up odd bookkeeping jobs, writing fiction, and trying to become a published novelist.

A Trend Some Can't Refuse

Carolyn, who feels more at home in jeans and a cotton sweater than a designer suit, voluntarily shrank her life, unlike those who have had it done for them when they've been downsized out of a job and paycheck. Obviously, the person who resigns feels more in control simplifying her life than the one who gets a pink slip. Deciding to uproot and cut back is contrary to the American style of "buying up."

For some the trade-off is about more than simplifying. Personal downsizing provides a chance for defining what you really want, cutting out not just luxuries but sorting through what doesn't ring your bells anymore. Having it all is another on the list of "shoulds." This set-up to want what others have leads to massive clutter and gets in the way of figuring out what you truly need.

Some women reach a point where they realize the stuff no longer makes them happy. They shed the old things, say thanks for the memories, and move on, walking lighter.

Marty, a publicist, has put her suburban house on the market in order to move into a co-housing development that she helped plan and build. This style of what's known as "intentional community" is part of a national trend, where people share mortgages, land, and much of their lives while retaining a small separate living space. "This is community, not communes," Marty says. It means moving into a duplex, giving up a large garage, big yard, storage space. The co-housing rules allow only native plants, which means no more daffodils in Marty's garden. And there's the privacy issue. "Since we'll be living so close to each other it will be a bit of a fishbowl. Harder to hide your bad habits." But she's gaining something a lot more. "Intentional community means friends living close by, shared skills and talents and resources, and a new house I helped design in a community I also helped design."

Marty is single and doesn't have children. At fifty she says she's tired of living alone. Through co-housing, she'll get an extended family and exposure to other people's kids. The idea of co-housing is not for adults to share in the child rearing, but to share in the caregiving. "It's like the old-style neighborhood," says Marty, "where everyone knew everyone's children and kept an eye on them."

She'll have less space to entertain in her new living room, but she'll have access to a large common house. Marty fantasizes about "a rainy night when I come home from work, have dinner, and then wander over to the commons. Someone will have built a fire. There will be people sipping wine and someone playing the piano." She pauses and grins. "Of course, it will be *my* piano." Marty's new duplex has no room to fit a baby grand, so she's donating hers to the group.

Personal downsizing provides a chance for defining what you really want, cutting out not just luxuries but sorting through what doesn't ring your bells anymore.

The Stuff of Life

"We had a housekeeper once a week. We lived very comfortably. I guess you would call us upper middle class," says Carolyn. "I had fifty pairs of shoes." The social life was full. Shows and ballets, concert season tickets. "A lot of what we did helped my work. I was good at networking. Even when we got married, I remember thinking that a lot of the people we invited were good contacts."

The life fit her image of success—at least some of it. "When I was little I thought I'd marry and have lots of children. I knew I wanted to make good money. I grew up in a poor family in Detroit. We were educated but poor. All the kids—there were eight—have at least a bachelor's degree."

She earned her living in the field of human services, where she invested her heart as well as her energy. Carolyn had started out in college as a math major and computer programmer, but an act of violence changed her direction. "I was raped. After that it just felt better to get involved in human services. I knew too many injustices in the world." She got a master's in social work, married, and took her first job, as program director for a battered women's shelter in Denver.

The Big Burnout

Carolyn chose the kind of career about which others say, "I don't know how she does it." Violence toward women and children became her focus. She started a self-defense class for women and moved up to executive director of the shelter. Then she opened the counseling agency with another therapist; they developed a good reputation among clients and in the legal community. Suddenly Carolyn was deluged, working eighty hours a week, making money but paying a huge emotional price. She didn't have children of her own, but Carolyn became absorbed in trying to fix other people's children. "A lot of them were cult survivors. They had unbelievable things done to them." And even though she was successful in helping them recover, the work became increasingly depressing. "I felt like I was living in a world of pain and violence. One day after I'd had a massage, all kinds of things came up that were locked inside. I got out of the shower that day and looked at the person in the mirror and said, 'You don't want to be a therapist anymore.' This peace came over me. My husband said, 'Great, now I get my partner back.' I was always so wiped out from my work, I wasn't much of a partner."

Good girls don't like disappointing anyone, but for Carolyn it went far beyond that. She worried about the women and children she would leave behind. "I couldn't just walk out the door and say 'bye y'all.' I knew some people would be angry with me. I was kind of a mother of the domestic violence movement there." She'd helped change the rape laws and was a leader in victims' rights work. She had helped a lot of people, made some important changes, and built a big life around all of that. But she was being crushed under the weight of it all. Carolyn knew she'd be no good to anyone if she didn't free herself. She announced she was leaving her practice at the end of that year. "I wasn't really sure what I would do. The word spread that I was quitting to open a flower shop. I heard that and thought that wouldn't be a bad idea." The human service community sent her off with a big party. "The sheriff's helicopter even flew over and shined a light down on my party."

She was leaving a life of accomplishment, public recognition, and financial success. And in the end, others understood and supported her decision to leave. But she wasn't sure where she was going. "I was scared about where we would go and how I would make money, but I never wavered. It was great though, because I'd even inspired others. At my party another woman with burnout came up and said I'd given her the courage to quit."

I was scared about where we would go
and how I would make money, but I never
wavered. . . . At my party another woman
with burnout came up and said I'd given
her the courage to quit.

Now, What Do You Want to Be?

"I always loved writing. I thought, 'I'll do that.' I used to write knockout reports. People would comment on how wonderful they were, how clear." Carolyn has started writing articles for a travel magazine that serves the coastal area, but it doesn't pay much and she is still trying to make the bigger time. She earns some money, and it's not a lot, doing bookkeeping for small businesses in her town.

She's surrounded by other voluntary downsizers who have taken the opportunity to enlarge their possibilities by shrinking their pocketbook. Many are people like her who moved from urban areas, some from high-paying jobs, and now find themselves living in their small ocean village "making money at things they never thought they'd do."

Carolyn, who describes herself as an "impoverished writer," still surprises herself with her detour. It was out of character to give up financial and job security and to pursue a field different from the one she'd prepared for. Good girls don't often take off in unexpected directions, unless someone else is driving.

> We thought we'd always live in Denver or some city. I had a good business, bringing in a lot of money. I always thought I'd do it forever. I remember once my husband asked me how long I'd do this kind of work. I said, "Until I'm a hundred." But we were out visiting my brother in San Francisco and drove up to the Mendocino Coast. We began thinking about a "back to the land" move. Then we found this place, on a ridge road with a view of the ocean. It smelled wonderful. I felt at peace.

Letting Go and Moving In

Carolyn wanted to make her claim to the land and also do a ritual to mark her ending and new beginning. The black candle was for releasing, the white for healing, the red for renewing. After her private ceremony she went back to Denver, put the house on the market, expecting it to take a year to sell because Denver's real estate market had plummeted. It looked like she'd have plenty of time for the transition. "I thought it would take a while. Two weeks later we had an offer. It scared the bejeebers out of us both. Now what do we do?" Things also fell into place in California. Rentals were usually scarce in their new town, but they found one in three days, a house they could live in until theirs was built.

Adjusting

Downsizing involves making new friends when you don't have the same professional contacts. A lot of women make friends through the workplace. When Carolyn was in Denver, her friends were other professional women. "We were all making decent money. We were all about equal in terms of jobs. The best thing we did was every month a bunch of us, kind of a support group, would go to the mountains and rent a condo."

When Carolyn moved to her new community she was looking for new friends. "I told myself I wanted to make at least one friend—a woman who I could bare my soul to and who would be there to stay even if we fought." She took a dance class and now her best friend is her dance instructor. It's an unlikely match but it works in her new world. "Deborah and I are solid even though we are completely different. She's from L.A. She's flamboyant."

So is the new Carolyn. The new friendship and town provided a fresh way for Carolyn to express herself, in addition to her writing. "In Denver I used to love to go to the theater and get decked out. When I moved here I hadn't quite gotten rid of the glitter in my closet." So she has started performing in dance recitals. As *a drag queen.* "It's so crazy but you have to understand that in Denver I had to watch everything I did, everywhere I went. I had to maintain a proper image. Here I've been able to let go of that. Performing is so much fun." And why a drag queen? Well, she says, because there are a bunch of men in the community who wanted to do a drag show, and she had all her fancy dresses and, she explains, "they were looking for a backup dancer."

For her fiftieth birthday she performed her drag act at her own party at a local club. "We all wear big hair and wonderful shoes."

> For the first year I felt a longing. I missed the hustle and bustle and old friends. Then I started enjoying being here. I don't do lunch in the city, but now I can go have lunch

and look at the ocean. . . . I like not being the center of attention, not being known everywhere I go. I don't think the limelight is that much fun. Sometimes in Denver if I wanted to go dancing with my friends, just get wild, I'd have to go out of state. Now I can be as crazy as I want in my own hometown. Going on stage, when the lights go up and we're in all our glitter with gobs of makeup and hair and people are screaming, I know what the Supremes felt like.

Her husband has decided to do a little scaling back, too. He was a captain but has gone back to being a first officer to get a less demanding schedule. "We do okay financially. But I haven't brought in enough income and that bothers me. Not him, but me."

She doesn't miss the life, or the sports car she traded for a truck, but she misses the control that her own money gave her. "Our money has always been separate and still is," says Carolyn, "and that makes it hard now. From the age of fourteen I paid for my clothes and books. Even after I got married, we had separate bank accounts and each paid a share into the mortgage. That's the only part that bothers me. I've always paid my way."

Still, they both enjoy the new, relaxed Carolyn. "My husband says I'm different. He says I stand up straighter than I ever did."

She's also noticed that she's lost the urge to schmooze. "I used to be a social butterfly and was great at small talk. I could flit through a party and never stop talking. I can't do that anymore. I can no longer make conversation about nothing."

Things That Grow in Small Places

There are as many styles of downsizing as there are motivations to do it. Claude and her husband live in a small stucco house in apple-growing country. It was a plain house that they found after giving up their family home, but they've turned it into a French cottage. Their garden is positioned in such a way that if you walk into the kitchen and look through the large, wood-framed window, the flowers look like a Monet painting. Most of the decorations inside the house—from colorful Guatemalan figures to French copper pans—are flea market finds.

Years ago, Claude and her husband made a conscious effort to cut back in consumption. "After our grandchildren were born, we decided that we'd rather put our money into their college funds than spend it on ourselves," says Claude, whose perspective on need and desire is colored by being a young girl in Nazi-occupied France during World War II. "I was entitled to one egg a month and one cup of milk a week. When I had both at the same time, my mother made crepes. I can't stand waste. It bothers me to see someone eat half an apple and throw it away."

The couple's simplified life allowed them to move from New York City to the country. Before downscaling, Claude was a laboratory technician at a hospital. Her husband was an art director for a national magazine. "It's interesting, more people envy us our freedom than they ever did our big house."

When they made their move they had been married for six years, but because of their work barely saw each other except on weekends. "We got to go to restaurants a lot, see some shows, and travel. But we wanted more of each other," says Claude, whose French accent makes their getaway sound even more romantic.

They moved with a camper bus full of as many belongings as it could hold and sold or gave away the rest. They lived on her husband's pension and a tight budget. Claude even made a lot of their clothes. "We did this so we could be together," says Claude. "And I've never regretted it."

Even after Claude inherited some money and could have started filling up their country cottage with new furnishings, they kept it simple. "I never wanted anything more. Possessions don't matter that much even though we love everything in this house. But if we lost it all in an earthquake we'd just go back to the flea market."

It's interesting, more people
envy us our freedom than
they ever did our big house.

A Room of Her Own

When her youngest son graduated from high school, Ruth announced, "I'm giving up housekeeping." She went back to work at a newspaper, starting as an editorial assistant and is now an investigative reporter and book author. She is as consumed by journalism as she once was by taking care of a family.

When her sons took off for college and career, Ruth was left with the four-bedroom house on a big piece of land, which felt even more unused after her husband died. Then she got a brainstorm. When one of her sons married and moved back to the area, Ruth suggested building a small rental for the couple on her property. "I realized that didn't make sense though. I should be in the honeymoon cottage." Now, Ruth lives in her little red house that is really only one room with a bathroom tucked into a corner. "I knew I could do it because I'm a bit of a loner and I have always thought small. For a while I thought about living on a sailboat or in a cabin in the woods. But now I'll never leave this place. It suits me perfectly."

All she took from the house was a table and benches, "the first pieces of furniture I bought when I married." She has room for her guitars and a wooden chest that holds the family scrapbooks and photographs. The rest, what she calls "the sentimental stuff," like her piano, is up at "the big house," where her son and his family now live. Ruth does very little cooking, keeping in line with her recent declaration: "I cooked three meals a day for twenty years. I don't want to do that ever again." Her diet is as spartan as her living accommodations. "Sometimes if I get inspired I'll stir-fry some vegetables in soy sauce. Or splurge," she says, "on a frozen yogurt." There's a deck where she can go look at the stars. And she knows all the trails into the woods. "I feel like Thoreau or John Muir in my cottage."

11

WHO TAKES CARE OF
THE CARETAKER?

Letting Go of Responsibility for
the Whole World and Taking
a Little of It for Yourself

*You who come of a younger and happier generation
may not have heard of her—you may not know
what I mean by The Angel in the House. I will
describe her as shortly as I can. She was intensely
sympathetic. She was immensely charming. She was
utterly unselfish. She excelled in the difficult arts of
family life. She sacrificed herself daily. If there was
chicken, she took the leg; if there was a draught, she
sat in it—in short she was so constituted that she
never had a mind or a wish of her own, but
preferred to sympathize always with the minds and
wishes of others. . . . Every house had its angel.*

—Virginia Woolf, "Professions for Women"

Someone Has to Do It

In another era, Adelle might have been a war nurse, quietly and tirelessly tending to the soldiers, going without food or sleep herself, fueled only by compassion in her commitment to remain everpresent to those in need. Near the end of the twentieth century, as the urban battleground began producing a new kind of casualty, Adelle created a different persona for the Red Cross angel of mercy—tending to a new population of the walking wounded with no rule book for how to go about it. She headed up the agency designated to handle the problems of mentally ill people on the streets after the state of California closed many of its mental institutions. She felt responsible for no less than each and every one of them.

Adelle is one of those women who inspire others to be their best. If you were to fall on hard times, she's the one you'd go to. Her voice reverberates with sincerity, and she carries herself with dignity. She embodies goodness. She has lived her life based on principles. If everyone lived like Adelle, the world would be a safer, more humane place.

She's a card-carrying leader in the club of consummate caretakers. Members recognize each other instantly. We trip over each other bringing food, napkins, bandages, small loans, a shoulder to cry on. In a roomful of caregivers no one is sitting down. We are up waiting to fetch. The person most responsible for creating happiness in the universe allows herself to be waited on only when injured, sick, or immediately following childbirth, and sometimes, if she's very evolved, on her birthday. Even then, the caregiver has to steel herself against baking her own birthday cake because, you know, everyone else is working so hard.

Adelle has taken a few lessons in how to care for herself in the middle of it all, and now gives hints to her friends. These days she not only is a role model for the good-hearted but for anyone heading for burnout. It has taken her decades to reach some balance. She talks about the answers she has found in her own life, and says the first step is asking the question. It's the one many of us ask, sometimes looking heavenward as though there's some cosmic solution: What are my limits?

We trip over each other bringing food, napkins, bandages, small loans, a shoulder to cry on. In a roomful of caregivers no one is sitting down.

Not Just Noblesse Oblige

Most of us who care about others want to help—whether it's giving time, money, or commitment to a cause. When it works it's something like the old "Stone Soup" fable where the poor person has only a rock in some boiling water, but convinces others that it's a healthy meal—if only each would bring a little something to put in it—and suddenly there's plenty to go around.

Some people do it in a big way, inspiring others. Perhaps that is why Diana, Princess of Wales, touched people so deeply. She brought glamour and a personal touch to the royal responsibility of raising money and awareness for causes from AIDS to landmines.

Other people do it in more quiet ways, giving a percentage of their income to charities, volunteering a few hours a week for a nonprofit service agency. There is always someone with fewer resources—emotional, financial, hours in the day—than we have. The requests come to us in small and big ways almost every day, and we're continually assessing how much we have to give.

How many boxes of Girl Scout cookies do you buy when that time of year rolls around? Which agency do you write a check to? Do you give money to the homeless person on the corner? How do you handle a needy friend, whose overwhelming personal problems take time from your own family? As a worker, how much of your personal security would you sacrifice to defend a colleague unfairly targeted by management? Or if you're in management, how far would you go to accommodate someone's family demands even if they're not doing their share at work?

When your children are struggling, how many of your other demands can you drop to just sit with them? If a mate is not doing his part at home because he has a lot of job pressures, how far can you go to fill in the gap before you're feeling martyred?

Some people can just look the other way and say, "No, I'm too busy," "That's your problem, not mine," "Too bad you're on the streets, but I have money problems, too," or "Do your share or get out." But that approach is anathema to women who instinctively want to care for others. Most of us are wobbling along the line between empathy and self-protection.

For women like Adelle, who have not only the instincts but a lifetime of Golden Rule conditioning, compassion can become a compulsion.

Help for the Helpers

Adelle's big challenge came when the state of California closed the doors to mental institutions in the early 1970s. At that time, Adelle worked for the Red Cross in Berkeley, California, where she had been in charge of programs for helping street people for two years. Suddenly, the number of needy people skyrocketed, as throngs of mentally ill people flooded into cities and towns unprepared to accommodate them.

> They sent thousands of people home to communities where they had no support. There were board and care homes, but mostly they provided board without care. The Berkeley Red Cross was the only program that said we could do something. We recruited a whole group of people and we did wonderful training. We assigned them all to people who had been released from institutions. We went out into the community and talked to these people. We asked, "Would you like a friend to come and visit you once a week?"
>
> The volunteers were quickly overwhelmed. People would come to us and need an equal amount of time as they were giving to their clients.

There were not enough volunteers to go around for the clients, and not enough Red Cross supervisors to go around for the volunteers. Faced with the need to do something with few resources,

Adelle and her colleagues put together a board to come up with solutions. They struck upon the idea of training the mentally ill people to look after one another. Their organization became the Creative Living Center. Adelle was the visionary behind the effort and she devoted herself to making it work. She immersed herself at every level of the organization, creating relationships with individual clients, inspiring volunteers to maintain their commitment, and handling the nuts-and-bolts business demands of a fledgling nonprofit organization.

Unlike the war nurses of old, she was not free to wander among the troops offering endless care through the night. Her work day had to come to an end, because she had other responsibilities at home. The mother of four teenagers and wife of a minister, Adelle had firm beliefs about her duties to family. Their home was a warm place, with a lot of music and laughter. It had long been a gathering place for friends, parishioners, and the children's friends. Now, there were six children living in the home, because two of her kids' friends were having troubles in their own homes and needed a place to stay. She could always make enough food to go around, even when the family fell on difficult times. There were hardly any scraps of food left after a meal, so careful was Adelle to conserve. One daughter said, "Mom was using the broccoli stems for stir-fry long before it was fashionable." It wasn't just economical to Adelle; she was raising her family to appreciate how fortunate they were compared with the hungry people on the street, and the starving people around the world. Everyone in the family gave 10 percent of their earnings to charity.

For Adelle and her family, *spirituality* was a verb—something you did, setting your own needs aside, until one day when she went to a retreat with old friends and started to cry.

> It had something to do with the size of the mending pile at home, and I hadn't had time to polish the silver napkin rings for months . . . and the client we took to the beach who walked off and we didn't know whether to go look for her or get everyone else home.
>
> I remember sitting at a table and telling people all these things. I opened my arms and held my hands out and said, "This is my picture of myself. There are no boundaries."

Putting On Some Armor

The self-sacrificing woman is one aspect of traditional femininity and is traditionally cherished most by those most served by her. It is the stuff of Mother's Day cards. It can feel like the best part of being human. Or it can feel like a one-sided relationship.

Adelle's tears surprised people who had always looked to her as a source of endless giving. Her commitment to others was a product of spiritual faith, and it was her turn to get some help. A friend at the retreat carried the biblical message that helped set her free.

> After I acknowledged I wasn't handling it all, someone in the group read to me from the Bible about putting on some armor. The passage from Ephesians is "Put on the whole armor of God so that you shall be able to stand firm. Put on the belt of truth, the breastplate of right-eousness, the shield of faith, the helmet of salvation, the sword of the Spirit." I envisioned myself doing that, cov-ering myself with that protection, protection for my heart.

Caring for others isn't something we want to let go of en-tirely, but it takes redefinition. There are ways to tell if putting yourself out for someone else feels right. Or if it feels like you're being taken advantage of, exploited, used up and treated like the proverbial doormat. Good girls have a knee-jerk response to give whatever's asked of them. Women who know their limits realize they must choose where their caregiving will have the greatest influence in the world—and the least drain on them.

Maybe it's about conscious caring. You decide who to extend yourself for and then it works for both of you. That's how it is with Lynn, who decided she wants to be the one on-call to drive her eighty-one-year-old mother around to do errands. "Then I don't worry about her driving," she says, "and we can both relax and enjoy ourselves."

I envisioned myself doing that,
covering myself with that protection,
protection for my heart.

Sometimes you have to figure out what your motives are. Is it that good-girl need to do the right thing, be popular, worried that if you say "no" to someone you'll disappoint them, and they'll like you less? "I think the hook for people who have so many needy friends is that way you always feel needed," says Jeannie, business owner and mother of two. "If you get enough people depending on you, you'll never be excluded or alone."

Some are more adept at avoiding the caretakers syndrome than others. Justine is a single mother and lawyer, who says, "I'm not likely to take on the care of a lot of extra people. I'm more protective of my privacy. If a friend comes to me with a problem and I'm overloaded, I can actually say 'I don't want to hear about it right now.'"

For Adelle, the drive to look after others is too strong to simply turn off. Nor would she want to. But she has learned, over the years, to measure the amounts she can give. Her transformation began at the retreat, and continued when she got home. When it was time to cook dinner, instead of cloth napkins in silver rings, she set a roll of toilet paper on the dining-room table. "That was a really gross thing to do," she says with a laugh. "But it got their attention." She talked to family members about their taking more responsibility around the house, and gained their understanding for how much her job took out of her. She also began opening up with a group of friends who met weekly for spiritual study, and would talk about the stress at work—"I was actually complaining, almost whining. It was a breakthrough."

Progress, she admits, was slow. Bit by bit she began to curb her compulsion to try to save the whole world. She started doing more for herself—vacations, travel, leisure reading. Somehow she was able to conserve her energy to continue fighting the good fight, without damaging herself in the process. Her armor served her well. Her personal light remained bright while she continued maintaining a sunny disposition for others.

When she retired, the city of Berkeley wanted to acknowledge all she had done. On her birthday, in 1993, the city leaders officially declared it "Adelle Lemon Day."

Of course, I can't shrug them off,
I'd feel like I'm letting them down.

Everybody's Therapist

Now that she's retired, Adelle still gets calls for guidance from former colleagues, but she doesn't always leap up to help. She schedules time to respond. She also still gets calls from former clients. But she screens them. "I have people who call me only for my listening ear. It's not mutual. There are people who call at one or two in the morning. Sometimes they're very aggressive. I just don't talk to them." She also has a game plan for walking down the street. Inevitably, someone will come up and ask her for spare change. Sometimes it's a former client. She used to find it impossible not to give money or a sympathetic ear. "Now I carry around a list of service agencies and resources, and I make sure they know where they can go to get help."

Empathetic women have to make choices. Mary, a lawyer with legal services, is still sorting out how to act on her innate feelings of kindness without being used up. Surprisingly, it's not her day job but her friendships that create the biggest dilemmas.

> Sometimes I feel like my job as a friend is to absorb everyone's anger, hurt feelings, resentments. I will tell them that I am not their boss or the teacher who has insulted them. I am not the guy who cut them off on the freeway or the waitress who ignored them. I am not the child who didn't call, the person who got them pregnant and made them drop out of college, so why are they dumping on me?
>
> It's because I take it. I have a big sign on me that says "Sponge Here. I blot up all messes and will absorb your wrath." Of course, I can't shrug them off, I'd feel like I'm letting them down.

Many women feel like Mary, the friend who hears everyone's sad tales but suspects that if she were to suddenly grab her heart and fall to the floor the friend would bend down and keep on telling her troubles. Mary wants to scream to the world, "I get depressed too, you know!"

Women, of course, have been conditioned by society—or maybe it's in their genes—to care for others. If it were a gender-equal quality, then we wouldn't make so much of caring, sensitive men. In most cases, you don't even need to qualify those adjectives for women; they come with the package. An uncaring woman is an aberration. Yet, we applaud the women in the movies who finally get tired of serving their ungracious lot. The classic scene is the husband who frowns one too many times over the meal placed before him and next finds it tossed in the garbage. Donna Reed turned Xena.

When Do I Get a Turn?

Barbara, a bookkeeper, and evolving good girl, found a better way to say "no" without having to feel like she had to give a reason. "Now I say, 'It doesn't work for me.' An old boyfriend taught it to me. That's all you need. You don't have to explain why. It's amazing."

But sometimes you can't say no. Izzy, twenty-seven, is the mother of a five-year-old and teacher of developmentally disabled adults. She doesn't have choices right now, but has to rely on her strength and sense of humor to get her through marathon days. "My day goes from 6:30 A.M. to 11 P.M. If you ask what I do strictly for myself I guess I'd say I eat. Okay, every night I give myself at least ten minutes to read before I go to bed."

Some women are squeezed from both ends of the family, raising young children while caring for elderly parents. This is not unique to a generation, but anyone who feels the pinch recognizes the label: "The Sandwich Generation." At forty, Natalie is the mother of a two-year-old and is dealing with her seriously ailing parents who live three thousand miles away. "I'm on the phone talking to my father," she says, "who is sure my mother is dying, and my little boy is out back trying to start the lawn mower. I chose it all. To have a house, to marry, to have a child. But sometimes, I'm so overwhelmed I dream of being alone."

There are extremes on both sides of the responsibility spectrum. Shea tells about rushing around, "five minutes late for soccer, trying to get my kids' socks dry, my motor running, and I look over at my mother-in-law who is in the garden with her friends. They seem to be in slow motion. They're studying some fungus and looking it up in their book. I think of all that I could do in the time it took them to look up a mushroom."

Shea's observation hits home to people on either end of the responsibility spectrum. Which would you rather be, running late for soccer with kids in wet socks or pondering a botanical specimen? The answer says a lot about where you are in your life. Shea was surprised when later in the day her mother-in-law said she was a little jealous of all Shea's responsibilities. "You are the hub of the wheel," her mother-in-law said. Be careful what you yearn for. Perhaps too few responsibilities may be as distressing as being overbooked.

I chose it all. To have a house, to marry, to have a child. But sometimes, I'm so overwhelmed I dream of being alone.

Me, Too

In the same year that Neva almost lost her husband to a heart attack, her son was hit in the head with a golf ball and went into uncontrollable seizures. The experience of almost losing the two people she loves the most in the world taught Neva not only to cherish their spared lives but her own as well. "I saw that things can be over just like that. For all of us, including me. And there are things I've been waiting too long to do."

After she got her husband on a healthy diet and exercise regimen and her son back in school and on an effective medication, Neva declared she was going back to her old love. She has started painting again after putting her talent on hold for years. She signed up for college art classes and created a strict working schedule for herself at her home studio. Even on family vacations, she says, "I go into the woods with my paints."

In addition to pursuing her art, squashed in childhood—"I was raised to believe that girls are only good for taking care of babies and a man"—she's cleared a lot of extras from her life.

> For years I did a lot of political work for candidates. I was one of those same faces always out there. Faithful, good Neva. Now, I only want to give my time to those things I truly believe in. No more candidates unless one comes along that really wows me. I'll go to their fundraisers but I'm not going to be working for them and walking precincts. . . . I've gotten to where I say this is my time, my life, and this needs to be my priority. I'm able to say, "I'd love to do it for you but I have work to do." And hope they don't think "selfish bitch." There used to be that nagging voice that says, "You can't do that." But I refuse to have that conversation anymore.

I've gotten to where I say this is my time, my life, and this needs to be my priority. . . . There used to be that nagging voice that says, "You can't do that." But I refuse to have that conversation anymore.

No More Slave for a Day

As Adelle discovered, your own house is a good place to start practicing letting go of the martyr syndrome. There are creative ways to share the duties. Holidays are ideal for experimenting. As hostess, you can give up being Slave for a Day.

There seems to be an unwritten edict that the person who prepares the holiday feast, fusses over it, and is the last one to get to eat it, is also the one who cleans up afterward. Virginia Woolf called her "The Angel in the House," the one whom she wrote was "utterly unselfish. She sacrificed herself daily. If there was chicken she took the leg; if there was a draught [draft], she sat in it." She is the phantom of the dining room, passing through to refill, replenish, and urge everyone to have more. She is the last to sit down. The first to get back up. Everyone else is eating. Sometimes the only thing she gets to chew on is her lip.

Back in the 1970s there were isolated actions to oppose this form of oppression. Some women defied tradition, refusing to wait on everyone else. Mutinous wives and mothers would remain seated at the table, munching on stray celery, idly picking the nuts out of the Waldorf, ignoring the crust forming on the potatoes, even engaging in real conversation. Often a woman guest would join in the conspiracy and linger with the hostess, both waiting to see how long it took for others to push back their chairs and dirty their hands.

But almost three decades later we know that the tradition of "let Mom do it" may be slipping back into the culture. There are still many Angels of the House who rate holidays by how much they suffer for their family.

Barbara, a liberated hostess, says the best part of Thanksgiving for her is sitting around the table after, "but I have a neat-freak mother and sister to contend with who jump to do the dishes as soon as everyone stops eating. My job is to ignore them, engage someone in conversation and not feel guilty hearing cleanup noises in the kitchen."

"Next Thanksgiving I'm going to call in sick," says Mary. "I heard my friend tell a guest that she never even tastes her food until she's putting it away. If I ever say that, shoot me."

12

SELFISH FOR A WEEK

Letting Go of Booking Others First and Scheduling Time Out for Yourself

She would not exchange her solitude for anything. Never again to be forced to move to the rhythms of others.

—Tillie Olsen

Leave the dishes unwashed and the demands on your time unanswered. Be ruthless and refuse to do what people ask of you.

—Lynne Sharon Schwartz

I think that wherever your journey takes you, there are new gods waiting there, with divine patience—and laughter..

—Susan M. Watkins

Aimless Drifting

The rafts drifted in lazy circles, coming to rest in a wide spot with a slow current on the Rogue River in southern Oregon. The women sat in a paddle boat. The paddles rested on their laps, white water behind them. There was no need for power at the moment. They had negotiated the rapids and were reasonably dry. On the two nearby oar boats, in which river guides did all the work, the rest of the boating party leaned back, long past feeling guilty about doing nothing. One sat with her arms stretched over her head, gazing at the sky. Another took out her journal. Some dozed and dangled their feet in the water. Had it only been three days since the overbooked other life was left behind for this stolen week of indulgence in nature, gourmet food prepared by someone else, friendly conversation, no TV, no phones, and the blessed, rare opportunity to do precisely as each pleased?

The eleven women on the trip had a few things in common. They were overscheduled, understimulated, and ready to be taken care of. It took them less than twenty-four hours to stop rationalizing why they deserved a getaway. There was nothing they couldn't leave for a week, they assured themselves, having lined others up to temporarily handle their responsibilities.

It takes a while to feel totally free. The first night they were patting their pockets to see if they had the key to the tent, and going through the mental checklist of everything left undone back home or at the office. Now they're laughing because worries are irrelevant. There's no room for an appointment book in a fanny pack. If you're deep enough in the river there is no cell-phone reception. On this stretch of the Rogue, there really is no easy way to turn around or change your mind and hitch a ride back to civilization.

The erstwhile guru was Rachel, the grande dame of this annual women's trip down the Rogue. Every year, Rachel brings the fine wine, sleeps under the stars in her silk negligee, and reminds the others to suppress their natural instinct to leap up and offer to help when the river guides serve the hors d'oeuvres. Rachel is the organizer for the trip, but she refuses to be considered the leader. Instead, she drew our attention to the quiet presence of the head river guide, Krystal, who oversees everything from cooking the entrees to conquering the rapids. Krystal has her own stories to tell and by the end of the week she shared some of them. But from the beginning she was the angel in charge of all creature comforts, giving permission to the group to be selfish for a week—starting with Rachel.

"Rachel's In"

She owns a bed-and-breakfast called Rachel's Inn on the coast of California and for fifty-one weeks of the year, she plays hostess to people who are getting away from their daily lives. But that's only part of Rachel's role in life. She has also taken on responsibility for no less than the California coastline, as the person most identified with the political movement to keep offshore oil rigs from going up in California. The joke among friends is that her bed-and-breakfast should be called "Rachel's In"—because she's always there, near the phone, available to respond to anything from a personal crisis to the latest political snafu. She finds herself at the center of things because she has the energy, brains, and pizzazz to handle both the work and the limelight.

A compelling voice in the Democratic party, she went to a Washington, D. C. meeting where she approached Vice President Al Gore, clasped his hand, smiled for the cameras, then met his eyes and quietly whispered between her teeth, "I won't let go until you tell me why you haven't signed the legislation to permanently protect the coast from offshore oil drilling." Her chutzpah is legendary. She is so bold in her drive to accomplish what she sees as right and good, that others rely on her. And she can't turn away from a cause she believes to be just.

She has brought her parents from the East Coast to the West Coast to live near her. Her father has Alzheimer's disease, and her mother has a heart condition. Her mother could not handle the debilitating effects of her husband's disease were it not for a day program at the local senior center. When the funding for the center had been cut, Rachel took it upon herself to help set up a fund-raiser, but few others were selling tickets. So she set up a table at the grocery store and sold them herself. She doesn't consider this extraordinary. "Someone had to do it," she says, the famous last words of the perennial caregiver.

But seven years ago, she began the annual tradition of the river trip. No matter what is happening, she tells herself—well, unless someone close to her were dying or the oil companies were to actually start laying claim to the coast—she will do this trip. As always, this time she leaves for the trip with loose ends. More tickets need to be sold for the senior center fund-raiser. She had sent off a fax to the secretary of the interior, and had not yet received the response. An employee at the inn had threatened to quit. She called a neighboring restaurant to make sure her inn's guests would be fed if her staff disappeared. She packed up her new pink tent, two negligees—a black one and a red one—enough California wine for eleven women for a week, and drove to Oregon.

> This trip is the one thing I do for myself. There's time and space to think about things without having to do anything about it. Everybody is able to be who they are without editing. There is so much judgment in our lives. "Don't do this." "Don't say that." Here, we give ourselves permission to just be. . . . It's loving and supportive, there's no competition, there are no "shoulds." If you fall into the water, everyone cheers that you did it so well.

Escape Fantasies

Especially for good girls bent on pleasing husbands, bosses, kids, friends, and everyone else in their lives, the self comes last. Talking about their secret fantasies for getting away from it all can be as intimate as confidences about love affairs.

Dissect the word "responsibility" and it means the ability to respond. But what about the ability to respond to oneself? Maybe it's time for an about-face on that Golden Rule. We may have been schooled to "do unto others as you would have them do unto you" but what about turning it around to "do unto yourself as you would do unto others"? Many women need convincing that they're worth as much effort as they give away to others.

Roxanne, for example, a mother, a graduate student, and wife, finds herself also looking after an ill mother. Her only self-indulgence is travel. She goes off to exotic places with her family, then claims at least an extra week after they return home to be by herself. Being alone in some faraway place and feeling that no one knows where she is is exhilarating. She cherishes this time like a starving person cherishes a loaf of bread. After one of these trips, she returns with a palpable memory of what it's like to be herself—alone, responsible only for herself and no one else. She begins to obsess over this feeling, plotting her next escape like a jail inmate desperate for freedom. One day her plight Krystallizes. She gets an opportunity to do a project that involves travel, away from work, away from her family. Even though it would be the realization of a long-held goal, she is wracked with guilt about the time it would take away from her responsibilities. She very nearly turns down the offer. But in her heart she knows that if she does, she will lose a part of herself forever. She knew she had to make some kind of change in her life when her escape fantasies began getting morbid.

> I actually fantasized about contracting the ideal disease, one that would make me sick enough to have to spend a few days in the hospital but not so sick I'd need an operation. Just to get a break.
>
> One day I confided this in a friend and discovered that she felt the same way. I realized that we already had a disease—too much to do, too much to worry about—and it's an epidemic.

We may have been schooled to "do unto others as you would have them do unto you" but what about turning it around to "do unto yourself as you would do unto others"?

Plotting Getaways

For women like Roxanne, talking with others is one way to identify the "I'm last on the list" syndrome and gather the wherewithal to make changes. Women find ways to schedule "getaways"—

whether for ten minutes or a week. They pressure each other to take care of themselves. For the women on the annual Rogue River trip, it's a commitment they've made so no matter what else is happening, they have to go. But there are less elaborate ways—a weekend camping trip, getting a group together for a pajama party in a motel with room service and a pool, going to the movies in the middle of the day. We're all finding our own escape routes.

Jane:
Stress has become hip. It's almost as though we're supposed to be overprogrammed.

It's something like "My Day-Runner is fuller than yours." The more overbooked you are, the more important you are. I decided to use my appointment book to my advantage. I have a new notation. It's "D.N." Someone looking at those initials sprinkled throughout the week might think I have a clandestine lover.

Actually, it stands for "Do Nothing." I have to schedule time for myself regularly to just flake off.

Cassie:
On Mother's Day, my family wanted to make me breakfast in bed, or take me out for lunch. I requested that they all get in the car and go somewhere, so I could spend a whole day in bed reading. They had a great time and so did I. So I suggested we do that once a month throughout the year.

Eileen:
My friend Donna threw a Women's Equality Day in August to celebrate women's suffrage. There was no menu. Women brought whatever they wanted, and Donna didn't care what it was. Everything goes with her barbecued albacore anyway. The idea was there's a minimum of organizing. The purpose was to get together and not worry about taking care of other people's needs. It was a great assortment of women and no one, not even Donna, knew everyone to begin with. We schmoozed. We ate. We drank and eventually we formed a circle and each told one thing we did in the last year that we were happy about. And we applauded each other. Some decided to sleep over, putting sleeping bags out in Donna's garden. Of course,

several of us lingered in the kitchen, talking and laughing. There was so much openness and acceptance. It was pretty magical.

Joy:
Sometimes I swap time-out packages with a friend. We mail each other *People* magazine or the *Star* or some gossipy magazine we filch at the dentist's office. If someone goes to the trouble of sending you something trashy, you're obligated to read it. . . . Oh, and there's chocolate we send along with it.

The ideal getaway has no practical value. It's being frivolous.

What's In It for Me?

The operative word for a great escape is "inessential." The ideal getaway has no practical value. It's being frivolous. Just for yourself. Reading a popular novel instead of important literature. Splashing around in the pool instead of doing laps. Having a meandering conversation where you exchange a lot of laughs but no productive information. Taking a bath, even though you had a shower that morning just because you want to feel warm water on your skin. Or, in the case of the Rogue River trip, having an outdoor experience without working at all.

Annie, a photographer, recalls how she was moved to sign up.

When one of the group invited me on the women's river trip, my first thought was "more work." I agreed only after I found out this was not a "macha" trip that I could justify as good exercise. You didn't have to paddle, you could ride on the oar boat, a Cadillac of the river, comfy and well equipped with good coffee and wine. Some women even brought cigars. If I was going to do something just for me, I wanted to make sure there was no other redeeming value than self-indulgence.

Banishing Guilt

When the women on the Rogue River trip had arrived at their first campsite, just before dusk, as the wine was poured and the cheese and vegetable dip miraculously appeared on trays before them, they looked up to see a kayaker paddling toward them. He was from the river boat company, arriving with a message for Krystal. He and Krystal huddled in an intense conversation while the women on the beach watched and held their breath. Just about everyone later confessed they feared the message was for them. One had asked the river company to find her if one of her ill parents became worse. Several had left the company's phone number at home in case of an emergency. For others, it could be a business crisis or trouble at the office.

Sitting on the rocky beach in their camping chairs, wine glasses in hand, they anxiously watched the exchange, starting to feel the familiar guilt nagging about abandoning their responsibilities.

Sensing the anxiety at the campsite, Krystal strode up to the women from the river's edge as soon as the kayaker went on his way. She smiled knowingly at the anxious faces, and nodded toward the kayaker as he made his way downstream. "He's an instructor. He just stopped to let me know that his kayak school was meeting at the next camp. It's fine. You can all relax."

Getting Perspective

The women occasionally looked with awe and curiosity at their senior river guide, Krystal, who without fanfare was helping shape their experience. Reserved and self-possessed, strong enough to maneuver the boat though slight in build, she was a study in natural beauty. Sleek-muscled, sure-footed, and able to get the assemblage to move, promising a waterfall ahead or an osprey nest, Krystal was an integral part of the group, but removed, too.

She was the woman who trained our eyes for this geological miracle of a canyon, such a visual feast that it was hard to decide where to look. Bald eagles perched in trees as we passed below. There were tree-covered ridges, each a micro-shade lighter green than the next. A nonchalant turtle sunned itself on a rock close enough to touch, nonplused by the slow-moving, three-boat fleet. Bubbles sifted up from some river-bottom activity.

> Krystal's selection was perfect on a river
> trip of women who all would relate to a
> book on "doing too much."

Krystal has served as the senior river guide for the women's trip on the Rogue for seven years. Some of the trip's regulars have been rafting with her for years. All of us wanted to know more about her. One day, as we drifted, Krystal reached out for ropes and pulled the three boats together in a cluster. "Time for your Thought for the Day," she said, holding the rafts together with one hand and pulling out her book with the other. Every morning since the trip began, she read to the group before they left camp. This morning they had packed their belongings into the blue waterproof river bags without the usual reading. But she hadn't forgotten. Out in the water, she pulled out her little book, *Meditations for Women Who Do Too Much* by Anne Wilson Schaef. The current moved close to the edge of the river. "Here comes another rock, ruining my moment!" she said with a laugh. Then she deftly used an oar to move her raft, and the other two rafts she held by a rope, away from danger. She breathed deeply, opened her book and read the day's message:

> Some of us find the words "obligations to myself" foreign. We have been raised to believe that we should sacrifice ourselves in order to be good.
>
> Then others of us have reacted to the female cult of self-sacrifice and decided that we needed to be selfish and to focus upon ourselves. Often we bounce back and forth between these two choices. Unfortunately (or fortunately, as the case may be), neither is satisfactory. Either way, we feel lonely, at loose ends, and unfulfilled.
>
> The third option is to honor ourselves. When we honor ourselves and give out of that honoring, our giving is very clean. If we are not honoring ourselves, our giving has strings attached and is uncomfortable for the giver and the receiver.

Krystal's selection was perfect on a river trip of women who all would relate to a book on "doing too much."

Self-Centered? Bravo!

Over the week, together we defined the umbilical cord–like connections we all make with the demands of our day-to-day lives. We could all come up with reasons we shouldn't take time out for ourselves, which were, of course, the very reasons we told each other we needed to.

One woman who adores her husband but felt the weight of his recent illness needed a break from the loving attachment that drives her to answer his every call for assistance. Two journalists who had been on a death watch with a woman who started out as a news source but had become a friend, had gotten her blessings to take a few days off. A woman who had rekindled a love affair with an old boyfriend worried about disappearing at this critical juncture but told herself the break was a good test of the renewed relationship.

One night, standing around the campfire, after the other women had shared their innermost concerns about what they had left behind to be here, one member of the assemblage gave a contented smile. She wanted nothing to do with the talk of deprivation. "I had no qualms about coming on this river trip," Judith said. "I'm very self-centered." There was a moment of stunned silence. Then everyone started to cheer.

It remains a mystery exactly why it was possible—in this group, on this river, with this guide—for it be okay to think, be, or say anything. Rachel marvels at the phenomenon of the river trip.

> At first I thought it was the particular group of people who were invited. You'd have a conversation, drift off, and someone else would come in. It was very comfortable and very supportive. Very nurturing. And that's not a cliché. At first I thought it was because of the women, but it turned out not to matter. It's the same with another group of women. It's the same each time, even though it's different. Everyone's allowing themselves to be open and undemanding. And we're all so happy not to be doing our lives. As she happily dips into a guacamole salad, she says, "I never eat avocados in my real life." A chorus of women correct her: "Rachel, this *is* your real life!"

Following Her Lead

In the early years, Krystal made it clear that she enjoyed being a guide on the annual Rogue women's trip. She would make sure she was the guide year after year and chose her favorite colleagues to be on her staff. Rachel recalls that at first Krystal was further apart from the group. There's always much to do, making sure the gear is packed, setting up the campsite, preparing the amazing gourmet meals—salmon with capers, fruit dipped in melted chocolate, Teriyaki chicken, peach upside-down cake, Sante Fe tacos—that materialize like magic when the ingredients emerge from big white coolers and are cooked over the portable grills. This is the first year that, in addition to her other responsibilities as senior guide, Krystal has taken it upon herself to read the Thought for the Day to the group.

On a warm afternoon, taking a hike up to a waterfall from one of the overnight campsites, one of the travelers learned that Krystal—the water warrior-nymph with waist-length auburn hair, muscles of a gymnast, and unlined, delicately featured face—was forty-five years old. That she looked ten years younger added to her mystique. It seemed somehow out of synch with the rhythm of the day to press for more of her story. But on the subsequent morning, after she chose to read a meditation about honesty, obligations, and honoring the self, the question begged to be asked. "Tell us about you, Krystal. We want to know how you came to be here, to work on this river." She told us her story:

When Krystal was twenty-five years old, she was the mother of a three-year-old and in a bad marriage that cut her off from others and felt dangerous. Her husband was jealous of her friends, suspicious of anything that brought her happiness outside of their marriage. "I found myself turning down invitations from other people, afraid of my husband's reaction should he find out I had spent time with anyone else. One by one, my friends disappeared from my life. I felt more and more alone in the world." Krystal got the courage together to tell her husband she needed changes in the marriage if she was going to stay. There were no changes, but she stayed with him out of fear, trying to find ways to open communication, express her desires, and assert herself. "He told me if I left, he would take our daughter away from me."

One day Krystal's father called and invited her to take a river-rafting trip on the Colorado River, through the Grand Canyon. That was her father's dream, not hers. But the prospect of getting away from the forceful control of her husband tugged on her. Although her husband had warned her that if she ever left, he would make sure she never saw her daughter again, she could manage a short trip.

"That's what I really thought. That I was just going away for two weeks." When she arrived in Arizona, she felt shaky and unsure of herself. "I didn't know how to relate to adults." But everyone was accepting of her, nonjudgmental and accepting. She felt free from others' expectations, no need to do or be anything at all. The skill of paddling came easily. She was an athlete, after all. And the stunning beauty of nature around her—the red rock canyon, the powerful rush of the river, the clear blue skies—was intoxicating. "I was literally in tears." The tears flowed from happiness, as she reconnected with something deep in herself that had been lost. And from sadness, that she had allowed herself to venture so far away from the person who she had been before her marriage. "It gave me confidence." She told the river guides that she wanted to come back and become one of them.

The Colorado River trip was an experience from which there was no going back. She had found her courage. She returned to her husband and announced she was going to leave. She had the will to fight for her daughter. Something inside her had broken free and there was no going back to the cage that had been her life for years.

Part of her felt she should stay in the marriage, regardless of the personal cost. "I felt so selfish," she said, invoking that familiar refrain. But she couldn't ignore her unhappiness and sense of hopelessness any longer. She left her husband and arranged a shared custody arrangement, so that she was with her daughter most of the year. For four months of the year, she was a river guide, a job she got by virtue of the fact that she had begged the Colorado River staff to let her join them. She learned to handle an oar boat and supervise a paddle boat with grace and strength. Soon it became clear that the four-month separation from her daughter was too much. It was then that she discovered the Rogue, closer to home.

She developed a passion for wildlife. At the age of thirty, she went back to school and studied biology. During the off-season for river rafting, she became involved in a wildlife program for rescuing injured birds of prey. She learned to give them physical therapy, massage their healing wings, and get them flying again. Her career became focused on giving freedom—to the birds she cared for and to the people she took down the rivers.

She exulted in the transformations that occurred among the people on her boats. "One family came from Los Angeles, unplugged from their routine of television and Nintendo. I watched the children growing more animated and happy by the hour."

Most people don't need to change their lives as much as she did to find their freedom, but Krystal has learned that most people need time away to evaluate their lives, see who they are, grow refreshed by nature and return to their lives with their selves intact. "There's something similar in watching a bird return to the wild, or people finding themselves again. I always want to say to them 'You can do it. If I could do it, you can do it.'"

Krystal's lament about feeling selfish resonates with people-pleasers who worry that putting themselves first is a bad thing. But doing something for themselves often turns out to be better for everyone. Krystal's leaving a bad marriage was a gift to herself that ended up creating a better environment for her daughter—plus the hundreds she's led down the river . . . and all those birds who get to fly again.

The Ending and the Beginning

For both of us, the lovely part of joining the women on the Rogue River trip was being with a group who had never met before, but who easily slipped into sharing everything from sunscreen to gripes to respect for solitude. If you wanted to sit on a rock separate from the others, no one called you in. On the other hand, if you wanted to compare glass ceilings you could fill a tent.

We indulged ourselves and got a little wild, going braless, telling sick jokes, and talking about old passions. Stripped down and minus our mirrors, we left behind our make-up, literally and figuratively, except for one mocha-colored lipstick that everyone ended up passing around. The experience was honest and spontaneous.

The Rogue River trip was an ideal way to practice fighting the current, going with the flow, and talking at the same time.

Negotiating rapids turned out to be an apt metaphor for the good girl's big challenge. The word *negotiate* comes from the Latin word for "ill at ease"—the very condition that most of us avoid. If we make it through the fear of losing our equanimity, we can claim the river as our own.

The last night, after we got off the river, we took rooms at a motel for showers, real beds, and phones. As we toasted each other at dinner, we spotted a mother at a nearby table with her husband and three children who kept looking over and smiling. We told her where we'd been and she sighed longingly, vowing to organize a weekend with her girlfriends. We loved that our group inspired another woman. That gave us an inkling of what our book could become: An inspiration for women to talk openly and pull each other out when we're sinking in our stuff. Of course, it doesn't need to be a river. A living room full of women will do.

We hope you've come away from this book with some insights. We have. After talking with some fifty different women in various stages of "becoming herself," we gained some tolerance. Judgments dissolved as we began to recognize ourselves in others, giving up competition in favor of empathy—"I've been there" or "maybe I'll get there."

See a woman acting particularly bitchy, gossipy, petty? Maybe she's back there on the bad girls' bench, acting out or having fun, creating a few boundaries for herself, rallying the strength to make her own way. Once we might have run for cover, but now we might allow her the "hissy fit." See someone being smarmy? Give her a ribbing, but add a pat on the back. You've been there, you understand.

The women we talked to seemed to intuitively "get" what *Goodbye Good Girl* means, but our friends breathed a sigh of "thank goodness" when we explained that we don't see bad as a goal, but as a step toward becoming whole.

In the end, we decided we like reformed good girls the best—conscious women who are genuinely collaborative, caring out of choice, not as an involuntary response. We had to tweak the word *good* to fit. We decided we liked good as in admirable but not dutiful. Good as in appropriate but not well-behaved. Good as in solid but not flawless. Good as in honest but not sappy.

But we'll stop now—before we create any new definitions that we'll have to live up to.

Some Other New Harbinger Self-Help Titles

The Headache & Neck Pain Workbook, $14.95
Perimenopause, $13.95
The Self-Forgiveness Handbook, $12.95
A Woman's Guide to Overcoming Sexual Fear and Pain, $14.95
Mind Over Malignancy, $12.95
Treating Panic Disorder and Agoraphobia, $44.95
Scarred Soul, $13.95
The Angry Heart, $13.95
Don't Take It Personally, $12.95
Becoming a Wise Parent For Your Grown Child, $12.95
Clear Your Past, Change Your Future, $12.95
Preparing for Surgery, $17.95
Coming Out Everyday, $13.95
Ten Things Every Parent Needs to Know, $12.95
The Power of Two, $12.95
It's Not OK Anymore, $13.95
The Daily Relaxer, $12.95
The Body Image Workbook, $17.95
Living with ADD, $17.95
Taking the Anxiety Out of Taking Tests, $12.95
The Taking Charge of Menopause Workbook, $17.95
Living with Angina, $12.95
PMS: Women Tell Women How to Control Premenstrual Syndrome, $13.95
Five Weeks to Healing Stress: The Wellness Option, $17.95
Choosing to Live: How to Defeat Suicide Through Cognitive Therapy, $12.95
Why Children Misbehave and What to Do About It, $14.95
Illuminating the Heart, $13.95
When Anger Hurts Your Kids, $12.95
The Addiction Workbook, $17.95
The Mother's Survival Guide to Recovery, $12.95
The Chronic Pain Control Workbook, Second Edition, $17.95
Fibromyalgia & Chronic Myofascial Pain Syndrome, $19.95
Diagnosis and Treatment of Sociopaths, $44.95
Flying Without Fear, $12.95
Kid Cooperation: How to Stop Yelling, Nagging & Pleading and Get Kids to Cooperate, $12.95
The Stop Smoking Workbook: Your Guide to Healthy Quitting, $17.95
Conquering Carpal Tunnel Syndrome and Other Repetitive Strain Injuries, $17.95
The Tao of Conversation, $12.95
Wellness at Work: Building Resilience for Job Stress, $17.95
What Your Doctor Can't Tell You About Cosmetic Surgery, $13.95
An End to Panic: Breakthrough Techniques for Overcoming Panic Disorder, $17.95
Living Without Procrastination: How to Stop Postponing Your Life, $12.95
Goodbye Mother, Hello Woman: Reweaving the Daughter Mother Relationship, $14.95
Letting Go of Anger: The 10 Most Common Anger Styles and What to Do About Them, $12.95
Messages: The Communication Skills Workbook, Second Edition, $13.95
Coping With Chronic Fatigue Syndrome: Nine Things You Can Do, $12.95
The Anxiety & Phobia Workbook, Second Edition, $17.95
Thueson's Guide to Over-the-Counter Drugs, $13.95
Natural Women's Health: A Guide to Healthy Living for Women of Any Age, $13.95
I'd Rather Be Married: Finding Your Future Spouse, $13.95
The Relaxation & Stress Reduction Workbook, Fourth Edition, $17.95
Living Without Depression & Manic Depression: A Workbook for Maintaining Mood Stability, $17.95
Coping With Schizophrenia: A Guide For Families, $13.95
Visualization for Change, Second Edition, $13.95
Postpartum Survival Guide, $13.95
Angry All the Time: An Emergency Guide to Anger Control, $12.95
Couple Skills: Making Your Relationship Work, $13.95
Self-Esteem, Second Edition, $13.95
I Can't Get Over It, A Handbook for Trauma Survivors, Second Edition, $15.95
Dying of Embarrassment: Help for Social Anxiety and Social Phobia, $12.95
The Depression Workbook: Living With Depression and Manic Depression, $17.95
Men & Grief: A Guide for Men Surviving the Death of a Loved One, $13.95
When the Bough Breaks: A Helping Guide for Parents of Sexually Abused Children, $11.95
When Once Is Not Enough: Help for Obsessive Compulsives, $13.95
The Three Minute Meditator, Third Edition, $12.95
Beyond Grief: A Guide for Recovering from the Death of a Loved One, $13.95
The Divorce Book, $13.95
Hypnosis for Change: A Manual of Proven Techniques, Third Edition, $13.95
When Anger Hurts, $13.95

Call **toll free, 1-800-748-6273,** to order. Have your Visa or Mastercard number ready. Or send a check for the titles you want to New Harbinger Publications, Inc., 5674 Shattuck Ave., Oakland, CA 94609. Include $3.80 for the first book and 75¢ for each additional book, to cover shipping and handling. (California residents please include appropriate sales tax.) Allow four to six weeks for delivery.

Prices subject to change without notice.